Behaviour Management

Peter Brett

Nelson Thornes

Text © Peter Brett 2002, 2007
Archive illustrations © Nelson Thornes Ltd 2002
New illustrations © Nelson Thornes Ltd 2007

First edition published in 2002

This edition published in 2007 by:
Nelson Thornes Ltd
Delta Place
27 Bath Road
CHELTENHAM
GL53 7TH
United Kingdom

07 08 09 10 11 / 10 9 8 7 6 5 4 3 2 1

A catalogue record for this book is available from the British Library

ISBN 978 0 7487 8182 9

New illustrations by Dave Russell and Angela Lumley

Page make-up by GreenGate Publishing Services, Tonbridge, Kent

Printed and bound in Slovenia by Korotan

With thanks to the following for permission to reproduce photos and other copyright material in this book:

p. 64 Brand X HC 274 (NT)

Cover photos of drilling, screwdriver, tape measure, marking with a ruler, and safety glasses; Measuring up, Activity, Did you know? and Safety tip icons; p. 1 and p. 9 all Corbis CI 183 (NT)

p. vii George Disario/Corbis

Cover photo of wood grain, Ingram ILR V1 CD2 BS (NT)

Page 150 and Fig. 5.4 taken by Martin Sookias, with thanks to Oldham College for the use of their wood machine workshop

Cover photo of man sawing; p. 41 both Pixland/Jupiter 178 (NT)

Figs 5.7 and 5.10 with thanks to Warwickshire College for the use of their furniture making workshop

Archive illustrations include artwork by Peters and Zabransky (UK) Ltd and Richard Morris, with colour added by GreenGate Publishing Services

Contents

Acknowledgements

My sincere thanks go to: my wife Christine for her assistance, support and constant encouragement; my daughter Sarah; grandchildren Matthew, Chris and Rebecca and son James and his partner Claire for their support, patience and sanity checks; my colleagues and associates past and present for their continued support of my work and motivation to continue.

Finally 'all the best for the future' to all who use this book, I trust it provides you with some of the help and motivation required to succeed in the construction industry.

Peter Brett

Introduction

National Vocational Qualifications (NVQs) in Construction

These qualifications focus on practical skills and knowledge. They have been developed and approved by people that work in the construction industry.

Construction NVQs are available in England, Wales and Northern Ireland. Scotland uses SVQs, which work in a similar way.

There are three levels of NVQs for construction crafts and operatives:

◆ Level 1 is seen as a 'foundation' to the construction industry, consisting of common core skills and occupational basic skills.
◆ Level 2 consists of common core skills and units of competence in a recognisable work role.
◆ Level 3 consists of further common core skills, plus a more complex set of units of competence in a recognisable work role, including some work of a supervisory nature.

Awarding body

CITB-Construction Skills and City & Guilds are the joint awarding body for the construction industry. CITB-Construction Skills is also responsible for the setting of standards for craft and operative NVQs.

Work roles

Each construction NVQ focuses on an individual work role. For example:

◆ bricklaying;
◆ site carpentry;
◆ bench joinery;
◆ painting and decorating;
◆ plastering;
◆ shop fitting.

Construction NVQ make up

Each work role is made up of a number of individual units of competence. For example:

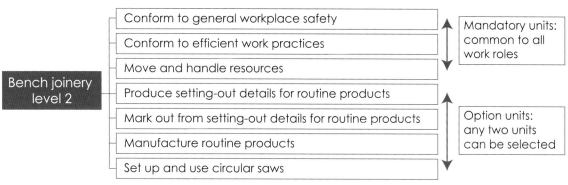

Figure 0.1 *Qualification structure*

All mandatory units must be undertaken plus a number of the options (two in the case of bench joinery) The number of option units in a work role and the number that are required to be undertaken will vary depending on the extent of the particular work role.

Unit of competence make up – in order to set out exactly what is contained in a unit and also make it easier to assess, each unit begins with a description. For example:

Conform to General Workplace Safety

This unit is about:

◆ awareness of relevant current statutory requirements and official guidance;
◆ personal responsibilities relating to workplace safety, wearing appropriate personal protective equipment (PPE) and compliance with warning/safety signs;
◆ personal behaviour in the workplace;
◆ security in the workplace.

The description is followed by a number of statements:

Performance criteria: these state exactly what you must be able to do.

Identify hazards

Scope of performance: this sets out what evidence is required to meet each of the performance criteria. The majority of this evidence must be from the workplace; simulation evidence is only allowed in limited circumstances.

Hazards, associated with the workplace and occupations at work, are recorded and/or reported.

Knowledge and understanding relating to performance criteria: this links in general terms the knowledge and understanding required to back up the performance criteria.

You must know and understand:

◆ the **hazards** associated with the occupational area;
◆ the method of **reporting** hazards in the workplace.

Scope of knowledge and understanding: this uses the key words contained in the Knowledge and understanding statements (shown in bold type) and expands them to cover the scope of what is expected of a competent worker in the construction industry.

Hazards:

◆ Associated with resources, workplace, environment, substances, equipment, obstructions, storage, services and work activities.

Reporting:

◆ Organisational reporting procedures and statutory requirements.

Collecting evidence

You will need to collect evidence of your satisfactory performance in each performance criteria of a unit of competence from your workplace. This should be inserted in a portfolio and referenced to each unit of competence. Evidence must confirm that your practical skills meet the appropriate performance criteria. Simulation evidence in a training environment is only allowed in a limited range of topics.

Evidence can come from any of the following people:

◆ employers;
◆ managers;
◆ supervisors;
◆ skilled work colleagues;
◆ work-based recorder;
◆ client.

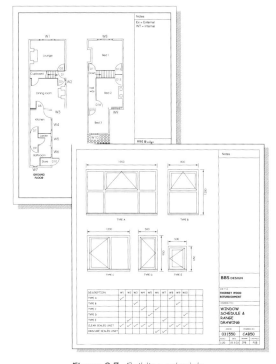

Figure 0.4 *Evidence of 'me' wearing PPE*

Figure 0.2 *Extracts from a specification*

Figure 0.3 *Building schedule*

Suitable types of evidence – you should include in your portfolio as much evidence as possible, from more than one of the following, for each performance criterion:

◆ Time sheets detailing the work you have undertaken; for these to be valid they must be signed by you and the work-based recorder.
◆ Drawings of the work you have undertaken; these should be supported by a witness testimony
◆ Photographs of the work you have undertaken, ideally with you in the photograph. To be valid, photographs should be supported by a statement containing a brief description of the work, details of where and when you carried it out, and be signed by yourself and either the work-based recorder, manager, supervisor, skilled worker or the client.
◆ Associated documentation used or produced as part of the work you have undertaken, such as specifications, forms and reports completed.
◆ Witness testimony – a statement by a responsible person confirming that you have undertaken certain work activities; these should include wherever possible a detailed description of the work you carried out.

T. Joycee Construction

Ridge House
Norton road
Cheltenham
GL 59 1DB

To whom it may concern:

I can confirm, that between 15 March and 8 November 2006 James Oakley worked on the refurbishment contract at The Rivermead Estate.

James was involved in the replacement of casement windows and internal window boards. He carried this work out to a competent standard at all times.

This work was undertaken in occupied houses, feedback from the tenants concerning James's communication with them and his consideration shown to their property, including the cleanliness of his work was always exemplary.

In addition James assisted me in the general day-to-day organization of the working environment, including the scheduling of the work and the safety induction of new staff. Indeed he always set a fine example by wearing at all times his safety helmet, boots and high visibility vest.

Yours Faithfully

Chris Heath

Chris Heath
(Site Project Manager)

Figure 0.5 *Eyewitness testimony*

Where an assessor considers your evidence as insufficient in either quality or quantity, you may be asked to undertake simulated activities in order to demonstrate/reinforce your competence in particular performance criteria.

The assessment process

The joint awarding body CITB-Construction Skills and City & Guilds approves organisations to carry out assessment of people for an NVQ award in construction. Typically these are:

◆ further education colleges;
◆ private training providers;
◆ construction companies.

Once approved these are known as assessment organisations. Their assessment work will involve the following personnel:

◆ *Assessors* – these are people who are occupationally competent in the work role in which you are being assessed and also qualified in the assessment process. Their role is to decide whether you are competent in each performance criteria. They will also observe you in the workplace to ensure you are carrying out the full range of activities to create the required evidence portfolio.
◆ *Internal verifier* – this is the person who is responsible in an assessment organisation for ensuring the quality of the assessments carried out by the assessors.
◆ *Work-based recorders* – these are people in the workplace who have been given by their employer the responsibility of authenticating the evidence that a candidate is collecting for his or her portfolio.
◆ *External verifiers* – they are employed by the joint awarding body to monitor the whole assessment process and ensure that each assessment organisation is working to the standards set.

How to use this book

This book covers the four occupational specific skill units for bench joinery at Level 2, separate books are available for the wood occupations at Level 1 and site carpentry at Level 2.

The mandatory common core units are covered in a companion book, *A Building Craft Foundation*, to which reference should be made.

These books are intended to be supported by:

- ◆ classroom activities;
- ◆ tutor reinforcement and guidance;
- ◆ group discussion;
- ◆ films, slides and videos;
- ◆ text books;
- ◆ independent study/research;
- ◆ practical activities.

You will be working towards a unit, one or more at a time as required. Discuss its content with your group, tutor or friends wherever possible. Attempt to answer the learning activities for that unit. Progressively work through all the units, discussing them and answering the assessment activities as you go. At the same time, you should be working on the matching practical activities in the workplace and collecting the required evidence.

This process is intended to aid learning and enable you to evaluate your understanding of the particular topic and to check your progress through the units. Where you are unable to answer a question, further reading and discussion of the topic is required.

Independent study/research

Browsing the Internet via a computer is an excellent means of accessing other sources of information as part of your research. Simply type in the website address of the company or organisation into a web browser and you will be connected to its website.

Try some of the following sites:

- ◆ Building Regulations: www.planningportal.gov.uk;
- ◆ British Standards: www.bsi-global.com;
- ◆ Building Research Establishment: ww.bre.co.uk;
- ◆ Construction training and careers: www.citb-constructionskills.co.uk and www.city-guilds.co.uk;
- ◆ Government publications: www.tso.co.uk;
- ◆ Health and safety: www.hse.gov.uk;
- ◆ Building materials and components: www.buildingcentre.co.uk;
- ◆ Types and use of timber in construction: www.trada.co.uk;
- ◆ Employment rights and trade unions www.worksmart.org.uk.

If you don't know the exact website address of the organisation you are looking for, or you simply wish to find out more information on a subject, you could use a 'search engine' to find the web pages. Search engines use 'key words' to find information on a subject. Enter a key word or words such as 'doors', 'windows', 'stairs' or 'strength grading' or 'timber', etc. or the name of a company/organisation, and it will search the Internet for information about your key words or name. You are then presented with a list of relevant websites that you can click on, which link you to the appropriate information pages.

Types of learning activity

The learning activities used in this book should be completed on loose-leaf paper and included as part of your portfolio of evidence. They are divided into the following:

- ◆ Measuring up: questions at the end of a major topic or units, which enable you to evaluate your understanding of a recently completed topic and to check your progress through the units.
- ◆ Measuring up questions are either multiple-choice questions or short-answer questions,
- ◆ Activity: An extended learning task normally at the end of a unit, which have been designed to reinforce your technical and communication skills in day-to-day work situations.

Multiple-choice questions normally consist of a statement or question followed by four possible answers. Only one answer is correct; the others are distracters. You have to select the most appropriate letter as your response.

Example 1

The mortise and tenon joint use between the stile and bottom rail of a panel door is termed:

(a) barefaced

(b) twin

(c) double

(d) diminished.

As twin is the correct answer your response should be b.

Example 2

The flight of stairs illustrated are called:

(a) open

(b) closed

(c) freestanding

(d) alternating.

As closed is the correct answer your response should be b.

Occasionally variants on the four-option multiple-choice question are used, as in the following examples.

How to use this book

Example 3

Match the items in *list one* with the items in *list two*.

List one refer to illustration:

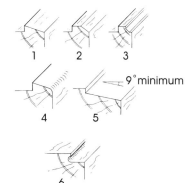

List two:

V. throat

W. chamfered

X. weathered

Y. splayed and rounded

Z. splayed.

The correct match is:

	V	W	X	Y	Z
(a)	3	4	1	2	5
(b)	6	2	1	4	3
(c)	3	4	5	6	2
(d)	6	2	5	4	1

This question requires you to work through the lists matching the items up (it is usual for the lists to be of different lengths). In this example;

V is 6

W is 2

X is 5

Y is 4

Z is 1

Therefore the correct response is d.

Example 4

Statement: Workshop rods should be drawn full size and not to a scale.

Reason: Timber components can be laid directly on the workshop rod for marking out.

(a) statement true	reason true
(b) statement false	reason false
(c) statement true	reason false
(d) statement false	reason true

This type of question comprises of a statement followed by a reason, where the both the statement and reason can be true or false. You are required to select the appropriate response.

In this example both the statement and reason are true, therefore the correct response is a.

measuring up

Short-answer questions consist of a task to which a short written answer is required. The length will vary depending on the 'doing' word in the task:

◆ 'name' or 'list' normally require one or two words for each item;
◆ 'state', 'define', 'describe' or 'explain' will require a short sentence or two;
◆ 'draw' or 'sketch' will require you to produce an illustration.

In addition, sketches can be added to any written answer to aid clarification.

Example 5

Name the intermediate vertical member of a framed door used to reduce panel width.

Typical answer: Muntin.

Example 6

Define the term 'weathering' when applied to joinery.

Typical answer: The slope given to horizontal surfaces to allow rainwater to run off, may also refer to measures taken to prevent capillarity.

Example 7

Produce a sketch to show the difference between a stuck and planted mould on a joinery section.

Typical answer:

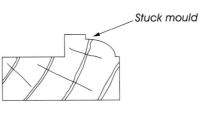

Stuck mould

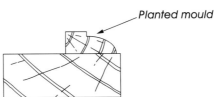

Planted mould

Introduction

These activities are a combination of short-answer questions on the same topic. They normally commence with a statement containing a certain amount of background information designed to set the scene for the question. This is then followed by a series of questions in logical order. The length of the expected answer to each sub-part will vary, depending on the topic and the wording of the question, from one or two words to a paragraph. There may be a blank form to complete, a sketch, a calculation, or a combination of any of these. At each stage the wording of the question will make it clear what is required. Blank forms for completion and inclusion in your portfolio of evidence may be downloaded from www.nelsonthornes.com/carpentry

Example 8:

The rear elevation of a door is illustrated in the figure.

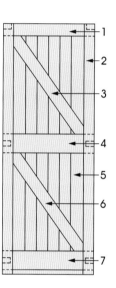

(a) Name the type of door.
(b) Produce a list that names the numbered components.
(c) Name a similar type of door that omits component 2.
(d) Make a sketch to show the exploded joint used between components 2 and 4.
(e) Produce a list to provide instructions for assembling the components in the order that they will be undertaken.
(f) On what edge of the door would the hinges be fitted and explain why?

Typical answer:

(a) Framed, ledged, braced and matchboarded door.
(b) 1. top rail
2. stile
3. upper brace
4. middle rail
5. matchboarding
6. lower brace
7. bottom rail
(c) Ledged, braced and matchboarded door.
(d)

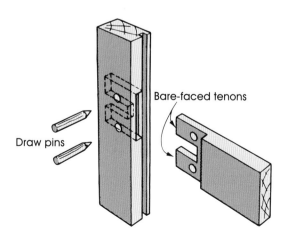

Bare-faced twin tenons

(e) 1. Dry assemble rails and stiles, check the fit of joints, overall sizes, square and winding.
   2. Adjust as required.
   3. Clean up inside edges of all framing components.
   4. Glue up and assemble rails and stiles, lightly drive wedges.
   5. Check square and winding; if all okay finish driving wedges.
   6. Paint or seal all concealed surfaces such as tongues and grooves, backs of rails and braces, etc.
   7. Fit matchboarding and secure by clench nailing.
   8. Mark, cut and fix braces.
   9. Finally clean up both faces of door and prepare for finishing.

(f) The hinges would be fitted on the right hand edge, as the lower ends of the braces should be on the hinged side of the door for maximum strength.

In addition to completing the learning activities, you may also be asked oral questions by your tutor, assessor or verifier. This is often done to gain further evidence of your written response or asked during a review of your portfolio to gain supplementary evidence: these questions normally take the form of; "How did you . . .?"; "Why did you . . .?"; "What would you do in the following circumstances . . .?" etc.

Other learning features used in this book

These include the following:

Colour enhanced **illustrations**   documents as an aid to clarity and reinforcement of text.

Mortise deadlock, latch or lock/latch

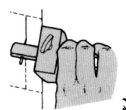

| Mark position on door edge | Gauge centre line on door edge | Drill out to width and depth |

did you know?

Adjustments to joints may be required if frames are distorted

did you know? boxes in the margin, which define new words or highlight key facts.

boxes in the margin, highlighting facts for you to follow or be aware of when undertaking practical tasks.

safety tip

Always ensure that the machine is isolated from the power supply before making any adjustments to guards, before changing any tooling, and before undertaking maintenance or cleaning down.

Worked examples included in the text for use as a guide when answering questions or undertaking other tasks.

example

Internal flight for a dwelling house with a total rise of 2574 mm and a restricted going of 2805 mm, assuming that the minimum number of steps are required:

◆ Minimum number of risers = total rise ÷ maximum permitted rise for location of stair (220 mm in this case) = 2574 mm ÷ 220 mm = 11.7, say 12 (each measuring less than the maximum permitted).

◆ Individual rise = total rise ÷ number of risers = 2574 mm ÷ 12 = 214.5 mm.

◆ Individual going = total going ÷ number of treads (always one less than the number of risers) = 2805 mm ÷ 11 = 255 mm.

◆ Maximum pitch (in this case) = 42°. Draw rise and going full size and check the angle with a protractor, see below. In this case it measures 40°, which is permissible.

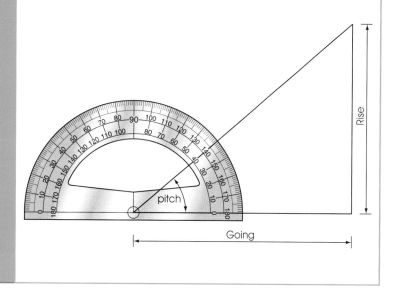

Underpinning Skills

This chapter is intended to provide the entrant at Level 2 with a review of the enabling skills and supporting job knowledge required to successfully complete the main practical activities in each of the bench joinery Level 2 units. Although its content is not accessed directly, knowledge of this is assumed and assessed in other units. It is concerned with the range of underpinning skills that are encountered on a day-to-day basis.

In this chapter you will cover the following range of topics:

- ◆ interpreting instructions and planning own work;
- ◆ adopting safe working practices;
- ◆ identifying, maintaining and using hand tools;
- ◆ setting up and using portable power tools;
- ◆ handling timber-based materials and components;
- ◆ recognition and use of timber and associated products;
- ◆ calculations.

You may have already achieved some or all of these skills and knowledge either in industry or as a result of training at Level 1 or similar. Thus, this underpinning skills chapter has been included in the form of typical questions for you to undertake. Questions are divided into topic areas. Where you cannot answer any particular question, further study should be undertaken using either the information source indicated, other appropriate textbooks, or talk it through with your tutor or a workmate.

This chapter should be studied on its own, or alongside other chapters according to your need.

Persons with prior achievement may wish to use these questions on underpinning skills as a refresher to support other chapters as required.

Interpreting instructions and planning own work

These two topics are covered in *A Building Craft Foundation* under 'communications' and 'materials'. These should be referred to if you have difficulty in answering the following questions.

1. State the reason why construction drawings are drawn to a scale and not full size.

2. What measurement on the 1:50 scale is shown in Figure 1.1?

3. Produce sketches to show the standard symbols used to represent: brickwork, blockwork, concrete, sawn and planed timber.

did you know?

The terms 'unwrot' and 'wrot' are sometimes used instead of sawn and planed timber.

4. State what is meant by orthographic projection.

5. Define the terms plan, elevation and section when applied to a drawing of an object.

6. State the purpose of specifications and schedules.

7. State why messages must be relayed accurately.

8. State the meaning of the following standard abbreviations:
   bwk   bldg
   DPC   dwg
   hwd   swd

9. State the action to be taken when damaged goods are received from a supplier.

10. State ONE reason why you as an employee should plan how to carry out work given to you.

11. Name the person you should contact in the event of a technical problem occurring at work.

12. State the reason why dust sheets should be used when working internally in occupied premises.

13. State why it is important to be polite with the customer.

14. State why it is important to be co-operative and helpful with work colleagues.

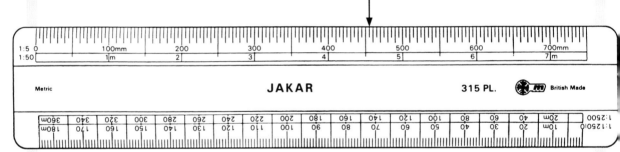

Figure 1.1 *Scale rule for question 2*

Adopting safe working practices

This topic is covered in *A Building Craft Foundation* under 'health and safety'. This should be referred to if you have difficulty in answering the following questions.

15. State TWO duties expected of you as an employee under the Health and Safety at Work Act.

16. State TWO objectives of the Health and Safety at Work Act.

17. State TWO main powers of a Health and Safety Executive inspector.

18. State TWO situations where protective equipment must be used. Name the item of equipment in EACH case.

19. State the reason for keeping work areas clear and tidy.

20. Name a suitable fire extinguisher for use on a flammable liquid or gas fire.

21. Describe the correct body position for lifting a large box from ground level.

22. Name the type of safety sign that is contained in a yellow triangle with a black border.

23. Describe the role of a site safety officer.

24. State the purpose of a toe board on a scaffold platform.

25. Define the terms 'hazard' and 'accident'.

26. List THREE checks that should be made before using a scaffold.

27. State the correct working angle of a ladder.

28. Briefly explain the procedures to be followed in the event of an emergency incident occurring on site.

29. The greatest number of fatal accidents in the construction industry involve:
    (a) falls from a height
    (b) being struck by a moving object
    (c) machinery
    (d) electricity.

Identifying, maintaining and using hand tools

This topic is covered in *Wood Occupations*. This should be referred to if you have difficulty in answering the following questions.

measuring up

30. Produce a sketch to show the difference in cutting action between a rip and cross-cut saw.

31. Name the saw best used for cutting down the sides of tenons to a middle rail of a door.

32. Define the difference between a warrington and claw hammer.

33. State an advantage of using a water level over using a spirit level.

34. State the procedure used for sharpening a plane iron.

35. When sharpening saws the following operations are carried out: setting, shaping, sharpening and topping. State the order in which these are carried out.

36. Explain the operations carried out when preparing a piece of sawn timber to PAR by hand.

37. State the purpose of using oil when sharpening plane and chisel blades.

38. Name the type of work for which a panel saw is most suitable.

39. Name the type of work for which a bullnose plane is most suitable.

40. Name THREE different types of chisel and state a use for EACH.

41. State the purpose of a bradawl.

42. Produce a sketch to show a mitre template and state a situation where it may be used.

43. Name a tool that can be used to draw large diameter curves.

44. State the reason for taking off the corners of a smoothing plane iron after sharpening.

Setting up and using portable power tools

This topic is covered in *Wood Occupations*. This should be referred to if you have difficulty in answering the following questions.

45. State FOUR basic safety rules that should be followed when using any powered tool.

46. When using a hand held electric circular saw state THREE operations that should be carried out before plugging the tool into the power supply.

47. State the reason why power tools should never be carried, dragged or suspended by their cables.

48. Describe the procedure for plunge cutting with a jig saw.

49. State the reason why the cutters of a portable planer should be allowed to stop before putting the tool down.

50. State how cutters are held in a portable powered router.

51. Describe the THREE basic work stages when using a plunging portable powered router.

52. Produce a sketch to show the correct direction of feed for a router in relation to the rotation of the cutter.

53. State the purpose of using 110 volt power tools.

54. What type of power tool does not require an earth wire?

55. State the correct location of an extension cable used in conjunction with a transformer that steps 240 volts mains supply down to 110 volts.

56. Which of the following sanders is best used for fine finishing work: circular, orbital or belt?

57. A cartridge-operated fixing tool is to be used for fixing timber grounds to a concrete ceiling. List THREE items of equipment that are recommended for the operator to wear.

58. The cartridge-operated fixing tool you are using on site has been supplied with THREE colours of cartridge: red, black and yellow. List them in order of decreasing strength.

59. State the action that the operator should take if a power tool is not working correctly or if its safety is suspect.

Underpinning Skills

Chapter 1

Handling timber-based materials and components

This topic is covered in *A Building Craft Foundation* under 'materials'. This should be referred to if you have difficulty in answering the following questions.

measuring up

60. State the reason for stacking timber off the ground.

61. State TWO reasons why materials storage on site should be planned.

62. State THREE personal hygiene precautions that may be recommended by a manufacturer when handling materials.

63. State the reason for using piling sticks or cross-bearers when stacking carcassing timber.

64. Give the reason for stacking sheet materials flat and level.

65. Explain why joinery should be stored under cover after delivery.

66. State the reason why the leaning of items of joinery against walls is not to be recommended.

67. State the reason why new deliveries are put at the back of existing stock in the store.

68. Explain why liquids should not be kept in any container other than that supplied by the manufacturer.

69. Explain why veneered sheets of plywood are stored good face to good face.

Recognition and use of timber and associated products

(1) Timber and manufactured boards

(2) Preservatives

(3) Adhesives

(4) Fixings

This topic is covered in *Wood Occupations*. This should be referred to if you have difficulty in answering the following questions.

70. Describe THREE main differences between softwoods and hardwoods.

71. List FOUR common sawn sizes for carcassing timber.

72. Softwood is available in stock lengths from 1.8 m. State the measurement that stock lengths increase by.

73. Produce a sketch to distinguish between multi-ply, blockboard and laminboard.

74. Describe what is meant by strength-graded timber and name TWO grades.

75. Produce sketches to show the following mouldings: torus, ogee, bullnosed, ovolo, scotia.

76. List the TWO initial factors that must be present for an attack of dry rot in timber.

77. Describe the THREE stages of an attack of dry rot.

78. State the purpose of using preservative-treated timber.

79. Name TWO types of timber preservative and state TWO methods of application.

80. Produce sketches to show the following timber defects: cup shake, knot, cupping, waney edge and sloping grain.

81. Name TWO common wood-boring insects and for EACH state the location and timber that it will most likely attack.

82. Define what is meant by conversion of timber and produce sketches to show through-and-through and quarter sawn.

83. Define the term 'seasoning of timber'.

84. State a suitable moisture content when installing carcassing timber and explain how a moisture meter measures this.

85. State TWO advantages that sheet material have over the use of solid timber.

86. A sheet of plywood has been marked up WBP grade. Explain what this means.

87. Explain the reason why water is brushed into the mesh side of hardboard prior to its use.

88. Define the following terms when applied to adhesives: storage/shelf life, pot life.

89. Explain the essential safety precaution to be taken when using a contact adhesive.

90. Produce a sketch to show the difference between countersunk, round-head and raised-head screws.

91. Describe a situation where EACH of the following nails may be used: wire nail, oval nail, annular nail and masonry nail.

92. Define with the aid of sketches EACH of the following types of nailing: dovetail, skew, and secret.

93. Describe a situation where a non-ferrous metal plug would be specified for screwing into rather than a fibre or plastic one.

Calculations

This topic is covered in *A Building Craft Foundation* under 'numerical skills'. This should be referred to if you have difficulty in answering the following questions.

94. Add together the following dimensions 750 mm, 1.200 m, 705 mm, 4.645 m.

95. 756 joinery components are produced by a manufacturer. 327 are to be preservative treated, the remainder require painting. State how many are to be painted.

96. Nine pieces of timber are required to make an item of joinery. How many pieces of timber are required to make 17 such items?

97. A rectangular room measures 4.8 m × 5.2 m. Calculate the floor area and the length of skirting required. Allow for ONE 900 mm wide door opening.

98. Five semicircular pieces of plywood are required. Calculate the cost of plywood at £4.55 per square metre if the radius of EACH semicircular piece is 600 mm.

99. A 105 m run of carcassing timber is required for a project. You have been asked to allow an additional 15% for cutting and wastage. Determine the amount to be ordered.

100. A triangular piece of plywood has a base span of 1.4 m and a rise of 500 mm. Determine in square metres the area of five such pieces.

101. A semicircular bay window has a diameter of 2.4 m. Determine the length of skirting required for this window.

102. A door 1980 mm in height is to have a handle fixed centrally. A security viewer is to be positioned 350 mm above this height. Determine the height of the viewer.

103. A carpenter earns £95.60 per day. The apprentice is paid 30% of this amount. Determine the wage bill for five days, for both people if the employer has to allow an additional 17.5% for on-costs.

104. Use a calculator or tables to solve the following:
    (a)   457 divided by 239
    (b)   6945 multiplied by 1350
    (c)   336 raised to the third power
    (d)   the square root of 183.

Setting out for Joinery

This chapter is intended to provide the reader **with an overview of** setting out for joinery work. Its contents are assessed in the **NVQ Unit VR 14 Produce Setting Out Details for Routine Products.**

In this chapter you will cover the following range of topics.

◆ design of joinery;
◆ site measurement;
◆ workshop rods;
◆ computer-aided setting out.

What is required in VR 14?

To complete this unit successfully you will be required to demonstrate your skill and knowledge of the following setting-out processes:

◆ interpreting information;
◆ adopting safe and healthy working practices;
◆ selecting materials, components and equipment;
◆ setting out details for internal and external joinery products.

You will be required practically to:

◆ produce setting out details for a range of joinery products including:
  ▶ doors
  ▶ frames (glazed and non-glazed)
  ▶ linings
  ▶ units and/or fitments
  ▶ staircases;
◆ produce cutting lists for the above range of joinery products;
◆ proportion joints;
◆ use setting out and testing tools;
◆ take workplace dimensions;
◆ communicate with other team members including machinists and joiners;
◆ undertake calculations for quantity, measurement or costs;
◆ requisition materials.

Design of joinery

A large proportion of the joinery used in the building industry today is mass-produced by large firms that specialise in the manufacture of a range of items (doors, windows, stairs, and units) to standard designs and specifications. However, there is still a great need for independent joinery works to produce joinery for high-quality work, for repair and replacement and one-off items to individual designs.

The design of this joinery is normally the responsibility of either an architect or designer, who should supply the joinery works with a brief consisting of scaled working drawings, full size details and a written specification, of the client's requirements. See Figure 2.1. However, these joinery details are often little more than a brief outline, leaving the construction details to the joinery works.

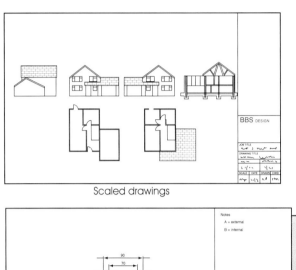

Scaled drawings

Specification

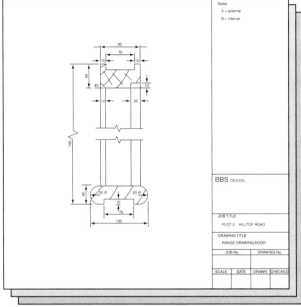

Joinery design details

Figure 2.1

The architect's or designer's brief to the joinery works

Often the best joinery is produced when architects or designers discuss their design at an early stage with the joinery manufacturer, so that each can appreciate the requirements and difficulties of the other and amend the design accordingly. This communication between the two parties enables the work to be carried out efficiently and therefore has a noticeable effect on the finished joinery item. In addition the joinery manufacturer may also be involved in the joinery design for small works directly with the customer when an architect or designer has not been employed.

When designing and detailing joinery three main aspects must be taken into account as illustrated in Figure 2.2. These are:

◆ function;
◆ production and materials;
◆ aesthetics.

All of these design aspects are important although, depending on the nature of the work in hand, more or less priority may be given to any aspect in order to achieve a satisfactory design.

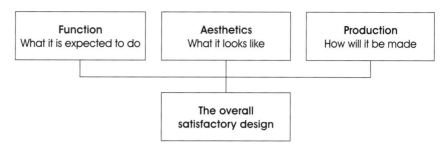

Figure 2.2 *Design considerations*

Function

This aspect is the first to be considered and concerns the general efficiency of an item. The designer will consider this by asking himself/herself a series of questions, such as:

◆ What are the main functions of the item, e.g. access, security, ventilation, seating?
◆ Who will mainly use the item, e.g. adults, teenagers or small children? Each will have a different size requirement.
◆ In what environment will it be used, e.g. temperature, humidity, weather, likelihood of vandalism, harsh treatment?
◆ What statutory regulations might affect the design, e.g. stairs, fire doors?

Table 2.1 *Functional design considerations*

Joinery requirement	Kitchen/rear access door and frame to new house
Main functions	◆ Access from kitchen to garden for a disabled person (wheelchair access required). ◆ Through vision. ◆ Daylight emission. ◆ Weather exclusion. ◆ Security.
Special functions	◆ Wider than standard door width (to accommodate wheelchair). ◆ Inward opening off ramp. ◆ Standard door height. ◆ Low-level glazing with clear glass (toughened) at line-of-sight when seated. ◆ Threshold flush with internal floor and outside ramp. ◆ Solid rebated frame. ◆ Five-lever security mortise lock fixed lower than standard height.
Environment	◆ Domestic usage (may take additional abrasion at low level). ◆ Adequate space both internally and externally. ◆ Aspect of door exposed to weather.
Special features	◆ Hardwood door and frame for increased resistance to abrasion. ◆ Kick plates fitted to both sides. ◆ Water bar at threshold with the minimum projection. ◆ Additional weather strips fitted to frame. ◆ Canopy roof desirable over ramp.
Statutory regulations	◆ See Building Regulations.
Design	◆ This is mainly fixed by the above specification. ◆ Materials requirements. ◆ Production requirements. ◆ Aesthetic requirements.

Setting out for Joinery

Chapter 2

An analysis of the answers to these questions will point to suitable **materials** and **construction details**, such as sizes and finishes, resulting in a satisfactory functional design. However, this functional design may require further amendment after considering the **production** and **aesthetic** aspects. This analysis can be applied to even the most simple or common joinery requirements. Although this can be a mental process, Table 2.1 shows a typical checklist for use as the design is committed to paper.

Production

This consideration is vital to the economic production of joinery. Construction details should be designed not only to avoid unnecessary handwork, enabling the maximum possible use of machinery and power tools, but also to utilise the minimum amount of material to the best possible effect.

Standard sections

The size and profile of a section will be determined by the functional considerations and the desired finished appearance. Figure 2.3 illustrates a range of standard joinery profiles, which can be economically produced by machine.

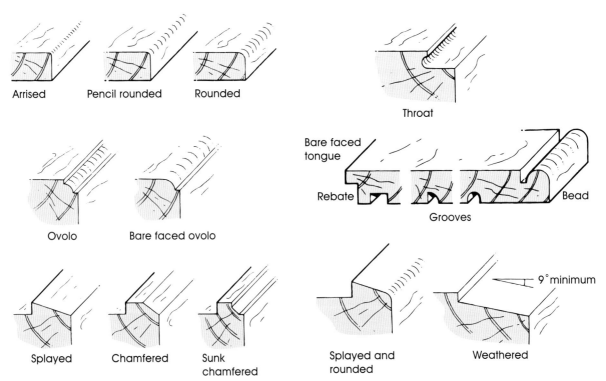

Figure 2.3 *Standard joinery profiles*

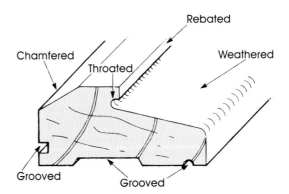

Figure 2.4 *Application of standard profiles to sill section*

Figure 2.4 illustrates the typical application of various standard profiles to produce one section. This may be described in a specification as a 'three-times grooved, once chamfered, rebated, throated, weathered and pencil-rounded sill section'.

The design and proportions of the profile should also take into account the type of joint to be used at intersections, as additional handwork can be involved at joints. Figure 2.5 illustrates a number of profiles and their suitability for machine scribed joints. Pencil-rounded and steeply chamfered profiles are best hand mitred, as the razor edge produced by scribing them is difficult to machine cleanly and is easily damaged during assembly. These problems are avoided by the use of a sunk chamfer or ovolo profile. It is impossible to scribe bead or other undercut profiles, so hand mitring is the only option.

did you know?

Hand mitring of joints is more expensive than machine scribing.

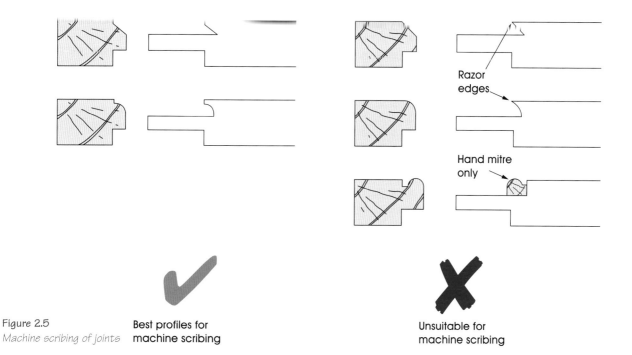

Razor edges

Hand mitre only

Figure 2.5
Machine scribing of joints

Best profiles for **machine scribing**

Unsuitable for **machine scribing**

Routing – an alternative to both scribing or hand mitring is the technique of routed profiles; see Figure 2.6 where rectangular sections are framed up and assembled, prior to being worked with a router.

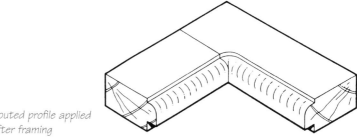

Figure 2.6 *Routed profile applied after framing*

Stopped rebates (see Figure 2.7) should be avoided whenever possible, as they are expensive to produce. This is because they require a separate machine operation, and also the curve left by the cutter on exit has to be squared by hand.

Setting out for Joinery **Chapter 2**

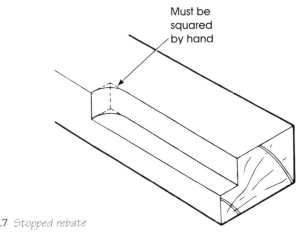

Must be squared by hand

Figure 2.7 *Stopped rebate*

Materials

Nature of timber

Table 2.2 *Moisture content for joinery*

When considering both the functional design and production of joinery items, an understanding of the nature of the material is essential. Timber is a **hygroscopic** material; this means it will readily absorb or give up moisture, depending on the surrounding environment. Before use, timber should be dried out to a moisture content that is approximately equal to the surrounding atmosphere in which it will be used. This is known as the **equilibrium moisture content** and, providing the moisture content and temperature remain the same, the timber will be stable. Table 2.2 shows typical moisture content ranges for a number of joinery situations.

Situation	Moisture content range
Internal joinery over or near sources of heat	6–10%
Internal joinery in centrally heated buildings	10–15%
Internal joinery in buildings with intermittent heating	13–17%
External joinery	15–20%

Changes in moisture content will result in dimensional changes in timber. Loss of moisture results in shrinkage and an increase will cause swelling. This movement is not the same in all directions; it differs (**differential movement**) relative to the growth structure of the tree from which it was cut. The directions of movement are tangential, radial and longitudinal (see Figure 2.8). The majority of movement takes place tangentially, in the direction of the annual rings. Radial movement at right angles to the annual rings is about half that of tangential. Longitudinal movement is virtually non-existent and can be disregarded. This differential movement causes distortion to take place in the timber. If it is remembered that in effect movement occurs along the annual rings, then the likely results of movement can be predicted.

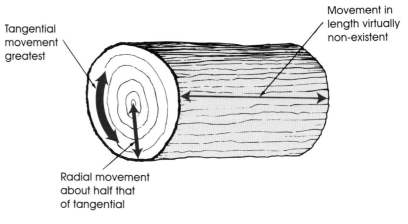

Tangential movement greatest

Movement in length virtually non-existent

Radial movement about half that of tangential

Figure 2.8 *Timber movement caused by moisture*

Chapter 2 *Setting out for Joinery*

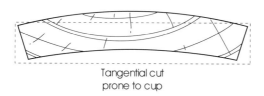

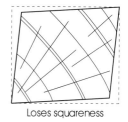

Tangential cut
prone to cup

Loses squareness

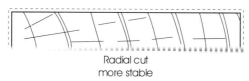

Radial cut
more stable

Shrinks but stable

Figure 2.9 *Different shrinkage in sections on drying*

Figure 2.9 illustrates the typical results, after drying out, of different sections cut from a tree:

◆ the tangential section shrinks much in width and is prone to cup;
◆ the radial section shrinks less in width and remains stable in shape;
◆ the square section with annual rings diagonal looses its squareness whereas, with annual rings at right angles, the section shrinks but remains stable.

Timber species – the amount of movement also varies with the species of timber. Table 2.3 lists four common joinery timbers and compares the amount of movement expected as the moisture fluctuates between 12% and 20%. It can be seen that a piece of European Redwood 100 mm wide would be expected to vary in width by 2.3 mm when cut tangentially, but only 1 mm when cut radially, as the moisture content moves between 12% and 20%.

Table 2.3 *Movement in timber between 12 and 20% moisture content ranges (mm per 100 mm width)*

Species	Tangential	Radial
European redwood	2.3	1.0
Douglas fir	1.5	1.0
Sapele	1.8	1.2
Utile	1.7	1.4

Design allowances for moisture movement

It is inevitable that a certain amount of moisture movement will take place in the finished item of joinery, which must be allowed for in design. The following are typical points of consideration:

◆ Figure 2.10 shows that wide boards show a bigger open joint as a result of shrinkage than do narrow ones. It is preferable to incorporate some form of feature that conceals the movement.

Setting out for Joinery

Chapter 2

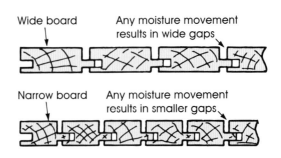

Figure 2.10 *Moisture movement in T&G boarding*

Bead   Vee joint   Sunk

◆ Tongued joints and cover moulds can be used to mask the effects of movement. Figure 2.11 illustrates typical situations.

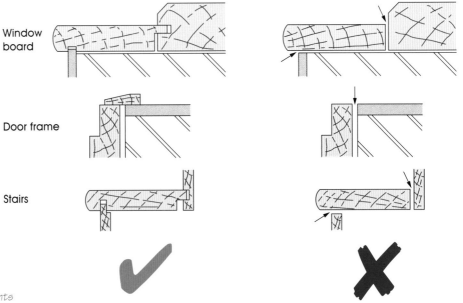

Window board

Door frame

Stairs

Figure 2.11 *Use of tongued joints and cover moulds*

Moisture movement concealed

Moisture movement results in gaps

◆ Wide tangentially sawn boards always cup away from the heart. Greater stability can be achieved by using narrower boards, or ripping wider boards and joining up with alternate heart-side up, heart-side down, as shown in Figure 2.12.

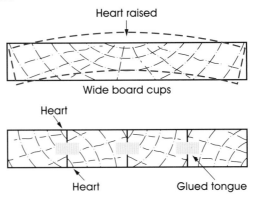

Heart raised

Wide board cups

Heart

Heart   Glued tongue

Figure 2.12 *Greater stability with narrow boards*

Chapter 2 Setting out for Joinery

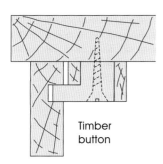

Timber button

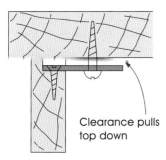

Clearance pulls top down

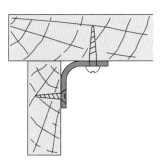

◆ Made-up wide boards, such as solid tabletops and countertops, act as one board with any movement taking place over the total width. The use of slot-screwed battens on the underside is desirable to prevent distortion whilst still allowing movement. Round or slotted steel washers may be used for added strength in conjunction with the battens (see Figure 2.13).

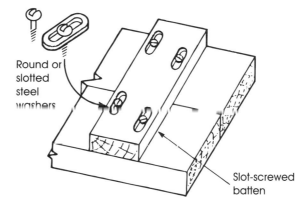

Round or slotted steel washers

Slot-screwed batten

Figure 2.13 *Slot-screwed batten on underside of solid tops*

◆ When fixing solid timber tops, differential movement between the top and frame or carcass should be allowed for by using buttons or metal shrinkage plates as shown in Figure 2.14.
◆ Figure 2.15 illustrates typical design points to be considered to allow for movement, when constructing cabinets in solid timber.

Figure 2.14
Fixings to solid tops, which allow for movement

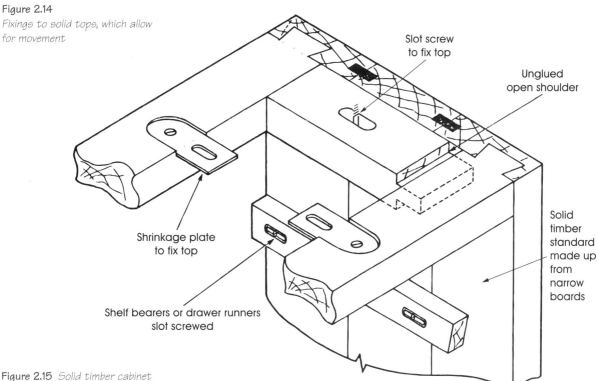

Slot screw to fix top

Unglued open shoulder

Shrinkage plate to fix top

Shelf bearers or drawer runners slot screwed

Solid timber standard made up from narrow boards

Figure 2.15 *Solid timber cabinet construction*

did you know?

The thickness of a tenon should be one-third of the timber's thickness, however it can vary slightly from this, to the nearest size of chisel available to chop the mortise.

◆ Tenon widths in framed joinery should be restricted to a maximum of five times their thickness. Wide tenons should be avoided as they are prone to a large amount of movement. The use of a haunch reduces their effective width, thus minimising movement. Movement at shoulders is avoided by using full length wedges or draw pinning near the shoulder. (See Figure 2.16.)

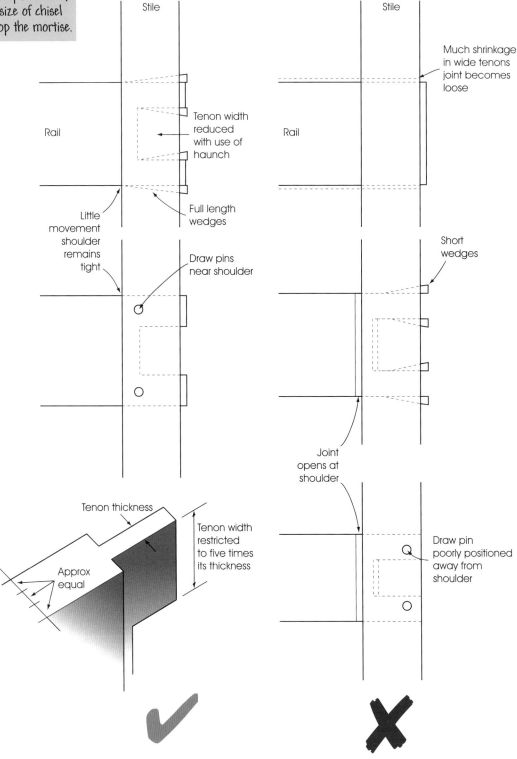

Figure 2.16 *Joint detailing*

did you know?

A bolection mould is one that is rebated over and stands proud of its surrounding framework.

◆ Bolection moulds should be slot-screwed through a panel in order to prevent the panel splitting. A planted mould used to cover the screw holes should be fixed to the framing and not to the panel. (See Figure 2.17).

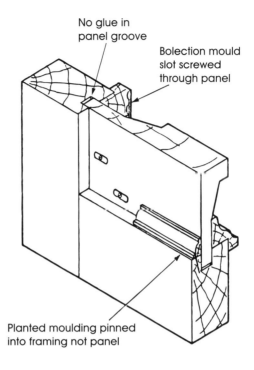

No glue in panel groove

Bolection mould slot screwed through panel

Planted moulding pinned into framing not panel

Figure 2.17
Fixing bolection mould

◆ Planted mouldings such as glazing beads and panel beads should never finish flush with the framing, as an unsightly gap will result. Figure 2.18 illustrates how they may be set back, set proud or have a decorative feature incorporated to break the joint.

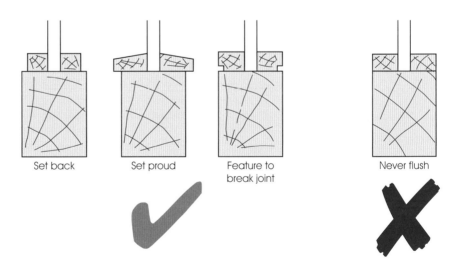

Set back   Set proud   Feature to break joint   Never flush

Figure 2.18 *Detailing planted mouldings*

Setting out for Joinery

Chapter 2

Weathering

External joinery must be designed to shed water and prevent capillarity, which would otherwise collect on horizontal surfaces and be attracted through fine spaces (see Figure 2.19).

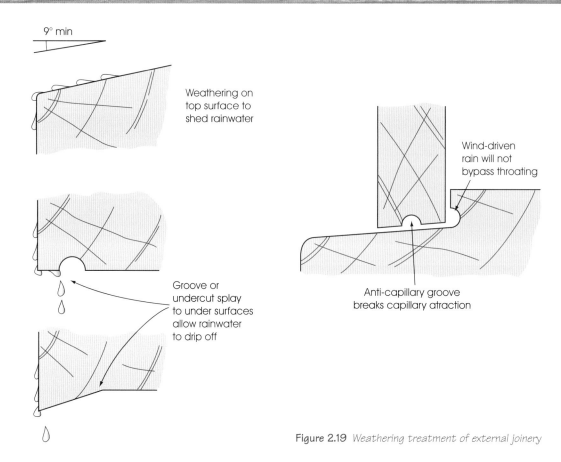

9° min

Weathering on top surface to shed rainwater

Wind-driven rain will not bypass throating

Groove or undercut splay to under surfaces allow rainwater to drip off

Anti-capillary groove breaks capillary atraction

Figure 2.19 *Weathering treatment of external joinery*

did you know?

Capillarity or capillary attraction is the phenomenon whereby a liquid can travel against the force of gravity, even vertically in fine spaces or between surfaces close together due to its own surface tension. The smaller the space the greater the attraction. Measures taken to prevent this are termed 'anti-capillary' measures.

- ◆ Top surfaces such as rails and sills should be 'weathered' or splayed at an angle of 9° minimum.
- ◆ Under-surfaces such as sills and cappings should incorporate drip grooves, or undercut splay.
- ◆ Where components join such as bottom rail of casement and sill, wide gaps are more effective than narrow ones in excluding water.
- ◆ The use of anti-capillary grooves and throatings in these locations is effective against wind-driven rain.

Key points

From these notes on the nature of timber it can be seen that careful consideration at the design and setting-out stages is required. Otherwise an item of joinery may quickly deteriorate, become unsightly or even become unfit for its purpose. The key factors that must always be borne in mind are:

- ◆ select an appropriate species of timber;
- ◆ specify an appropriate method of conversion;
- ◆ specify an appropriate moisture content (this must be maintained during production and delivery);
- ◆ use construction details that both minimise effects of movement, yet allow movement to take place without damage.

Aesthetics

This is concerned with the appearance or 'beauty' of an item and can thus be down to individual opinion. What is in good taste or acceptable to one person may be the complete opposite to another.

The aesthetics of joinery is the province of the architect or designer who has a sensitive trained eye and can consider the complexities of proportion, shape, harmony, finish and compatibility to produce a design that will have the desired effect.

In addition, the aesthetic effect can be considerably enhanced or marred in the joinery works by the degree of enthusiasm and craftsmanship exercised by the machinist and joiner during each stage of manufacture and installation.

Many joinery works operate an internal quality control procedure, whereby the joiners are responsible for checking their own work on completion and attaching a quality label to it. Figure 2.20 illustrates a typical quality label, which identifies the job and the person undertaking the checks. In addition to the quality checks undertaken by the joiner, random sample quality checks are normally carried out by a foreman or manager on a daily or regular basis. This provides a further quality-control measure.

A typical company's quality-check sheet for joinery assembly work is shown in Figure 2.21. It contains guidance for making the quality check and includes a grading system, which can be used as statistical quality evidence.

BBS
Quality Assured Joinery

Another Quality Joinery Product
Supplied by BBS. Tel. 01159434343

Part No. _____ Date. _____
Description._____
Order No. _____
Checked by. _____

Figure 2.20 *Quality check label*

BBS Quality Assured Joinery

JOINERY STANDARDS

- ❑ All joinery, units and subassemblies to be clean and free of shavings etc.
- ❑ All items to be free of surplus glue.
- ❑ All seen surfaces and edges to be free from scratches and blemishes.
- ❑ All seen surfaces and edges to be free from machine marks and excessive sanding marks. No cross-grain sanding marks on clear finished work.
- ❑ All joints and mitres to be tight fitting.
- ❑ All sharp arrises to be removed.
- ❑ All glass, mirrors and other brightwork to be cleaned and smear free.
- ❑ All doors, drawers and other moving parts should operate smoothly.
- ❑ All ironmongery should operate correctly.
- ❑ All dimensions to be within + or – 1 mm.
- ❑ All items to be square where applicable.
- ❑ All finished items should conform to all details supplied.
- ❑ All finished items should carry a completed quality label.

Quality control check percentage rating

ELEMENT	CONFORMS		Non-conforming
	YES	NO	Reduction %
Overall dimensions and squareness			–10%
Joints and mitres			–10%
Door and drawer operation			–10%
Ironmongery operation			–5%
Surface and edge finish			–10%
Cleanliness			–3%
Correct to detail			–10%
Quality label			–3%
	Total Rating		%

Comments:

Inspected by:_____ Date:_____

Figure 2.21 *Typical quality check sheet*

---

did you know?

You are responsible for quality – get it right first time!

Site measurement

Before working drawings and rods can be produced, it is often necessary to make a site survey to check the actual measurements. It is preferable for this to be carried out by the joinery manufacturer's setter-out, since it is he or she who will later use the information when setting out the rod, deciding the allowances to be made for fitting and fixing, in addition to maximum made-up sizes for access.

Joinery items for existing buildings and rehabilitation work will always require a site survey, whereas the need for a site survey for joinery in new buildings will depend on the specification.

did you know?

Rods are full-size working drawings of an item of joinery, which are used when marking out.

Specification methods

The two main methods of specifying joinery items are:

◆ *Built-in joinery* – where the joinery item is specified as 'built-in' or positioned during the main construction process, the work can normally be carried out directly from the architect's drawings and specifications without any need to take site dimensions. In many cases these may not even exist at the time.
◆ *Fixed-in joinery* – in cases where the joinery item is specified as 'fixed-in' or inserted in position after the main construction process, it is the joinery manufacturer's responsibility to take all measurements required for the item from the building and not the architect's drawings.

The extent of the measurements and details taken during the site survey will depend on the nature of the work in hand. It can clearly be seen that the requirements of a survey for a small reception desk in a new building will be completely different from those of a survey for the complete refurbishment of an existing office block. The details taken may range from a single dimensioned sketch to a full external and internal survey of the whole building.

Survey procedure

Each survey is considered separately, and sufficient measurements and details are taken in order to fulfil the survey's specific requirements. However a methodical approach is always required to avoid later confusion. The following survey procedures can be used to advantage in most circumstances.

Drawings – the floor plans and details supplied by the architect for joinery items will form the basis of the survey. The relevant measurements, etc. are taken and recorded on these. Before the actual survey, the building should be looked over, both internally and externally to determine its general layout and any likely difficulties.

External survey – sketch an outline plan and elevations of the building and then add the measurements. Wherever possible running dimensions are preferred to separate dimensions for plans, since an error made in recording one separate dimension will throw all succeeding dimensions out of place and also make the total length incorrect (see Figure 2.22).

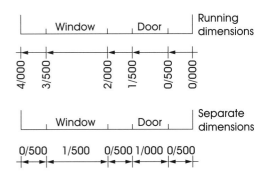

Figure 2.22 *Outline dimensions*

Running dimensions are recorded at right angles to the line, an arrowhead indicating each cumulative point. To avoid confusing the position of the decimal point an oblique stroke is used to separate metres and millimetres. **Separate dimensions** are recorded on the line, its extent being indicated by arrowheads at either end.

It is important that this distinction between the two methods is observed, because in certain situations it may be necessary to use both on the same sketch. Typical external survey sketches are shown in Figure 2.23.

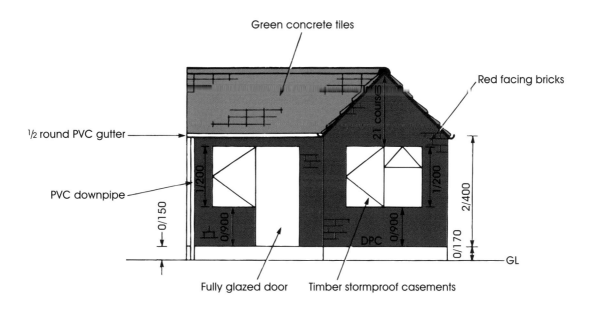

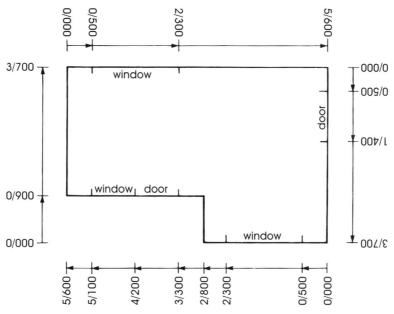

Figure 2.23 *Typical external survey sketches*

Running dimensions are taken in a clockwise direction around the building. Vertical dimensions on the elevations are taken from a level datum, often the damp proof course. Where measurements cannot be taken because they are inaccessible, they can be estimated by counting the brick courses and relating this to brickwork lower down that can be accurately measured.

All external details of materials and finishes, etc. should be recorded on the elevation sketches.

Where the survey is for a shop front or similar, accurate dimensions of the opening will be required. Vertical measurements should be taken at either end and at a number of intermediate positions. Horizontal measurements at the top and bottom are required. The diagonals should be taken to check the squareness and accuracy of the opening. Also, the reveals should be checked for plumb and straightness (see Figure 2.24).

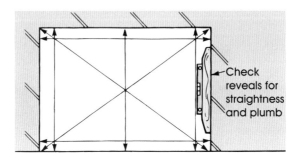

Figure 2.24 *Measuring an opening*

In addition, the head of the opening should also be checked for level and the slope of the pavement or exterior surface measured. The slope can be determined by means of a long straight edge, spirit level and rule as shown in Figure 2.25. Where the opening is too wide, the slope can be measured in several stages using the same method.

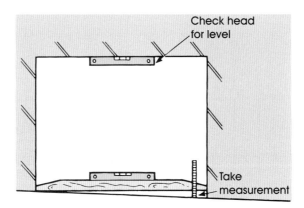

Figure 2.25 *Checking slope of ground across an opening*

Photographs of the elevations are often taken as a backup to the sketches, especially for fine or intricate details.

Internal survey – dimensioned sketches are made of each floor or room starting at ground level. These sketches are traced from the external outline plan of the building, measuring through door or window openings to determine the thickness of the walls. Each floor plan should show a horizontal section through the building, about 1 m above floor level. Measurements should be taken and recorded on the sketches in a clockwise direction around each room. Diagonal measurements from corner to corner check the shape of the room and enable one to redraw it later. Floor-to-ceiling heights are circled in the centre of each room. Floor construction and partition wall details are also shown on the floor plans. The floorboards run at right angles to the span of floor joists. The lines of nails indicate joist spacing (see Figure 2.26).

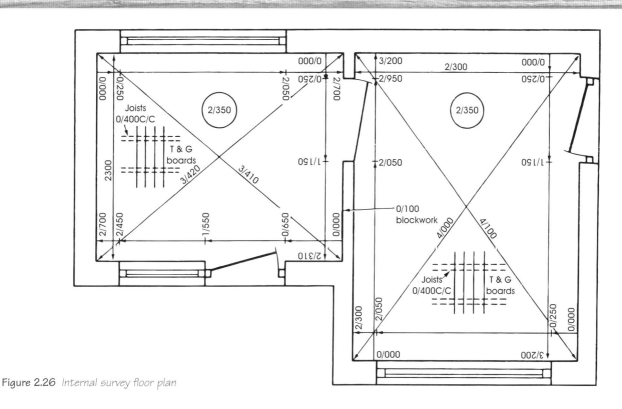

Figure 2.26 *Internal survey floor plan*

did you know?

Circled dimensions on floor plans usually indicate floor to ceiling heights.

Pattern staining on walls and ceilings can sometimes indicate positions of grounds or battening and ceiling joists (see Figure 2.27).

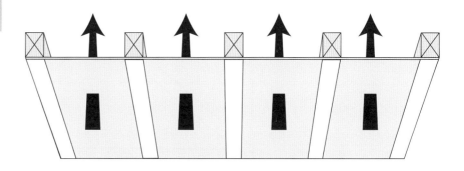

Figure 2.27 *Pattern staining can indicate position of timber behind*

did you know?

Pattern staining is a discolouration of wall or ceiling surfaces showing the structure behind. It is caused by the fact that the colder spaces between joists, studs or battens conduct more heat than the timber component, as heat is conducted through dust, and dirt in the air is left on the surface resulting in a stained appearance.

Walls can be identified by sounding them. When tapped with the fist, brick walls sound solid, thin blockwork walls tend to vibrate, and stud walls sound solid over the studs and hollow between them. Walls should also be checked for straightness and plumb, and any irregularities noted.

Where joinery items are to be repaired or replaced, full-sized details of the sections and mouldings must be made to allow them to be matched later at the workshop. This task can be eased considerably by the use of a moulding template. The pins of the template are pressed into the contours of the moulding. It is then placed on the sketchpad and drawn around (see Figure 2.28).

The exact location from which the moulding is taken should be noted as this may vary from room to room.

Setting out for Joinery

Chapter 2

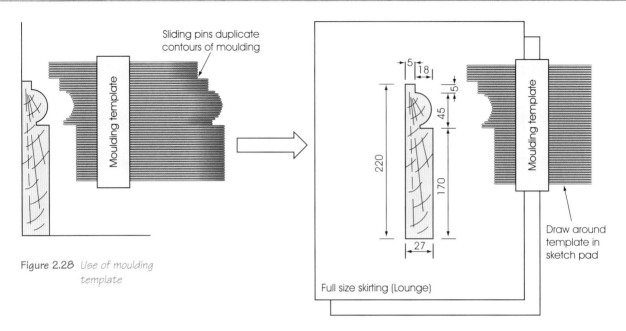

Figure 2.28 *Use of moulding template*

Full size skirting (Lounge)

Using sketches – sketches of internal elevations or photographs may be required especially where intricate details are concerned.

Sketches of the vertical sections taken at right angles to the building's external walls complete the main sketches. A typical section is shown in Figure 2.29. Sections should include door and window heights, as well as the internal height of the roof. The thickness of upper floors and ceilings can be measured at the stairwell or loft trap-door opening.

Only details that can be seen and measured are sketched. No attempt should be made to guess details, so foundations, floor construction and lintels, etc. are not shown.

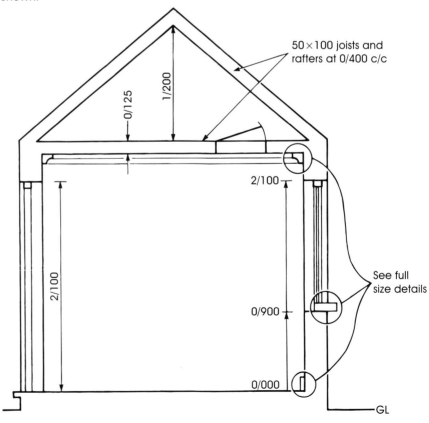

Figure 2.29 *Vertical section sketch*

Using datum lines – it is often advantageous, particularly in large areas, to establish a datum line around the interior at this stage. They should be indicated thus: ⍓

The datum line is established at a convenient height (about 1 m above the finished floor level). From this position all height measurements may then be taken, up or down as required. This reveals any differences in the floor to ceiling heights, any slope in the floor or ceiling, as well as the heights of the openings and beams, etc. as shown in Figure 2.30.

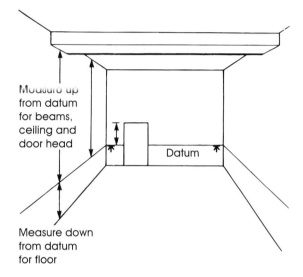

Measure up from datum for beams, ceiling and door head

Datum

Measure down from datum for floor

Figure 2.30 *Use of a datum line*

To establish the datum line, transfer a level position to each corner of the room using a water level as shown in Figure 2.31. Having established the corner positions, stretch a chalk line between each of the two marks in turn and spring it in the middle, leaving a horizontal chalk-dust line on the wall. The water level must be prepared well in advance of using it. This is done by filling it from one end with water, taking care not to trap any air bubbles. Check by holding up the two glass tubes side by side. The levels of the water should settle at the same height. Alternatively, an optical or laser level may be used to establish the datum.

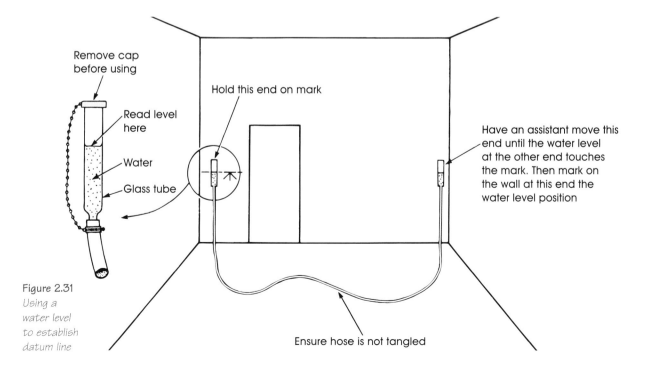

Remove cap before using

Read level here

Water

Glass tube

Hold this end on mark

Have an assistant move this end until the water level at the other end touches the mark. Then mark on the wall at this end the water level position

Ensure hose is not tangled

Figure 2.31
Using a water level to establish datum line

Setting out for Joinery

Chapter 2

Specifying stairs – where a new flight of stairs is required the total rise and total going should be measured.

The total rise is the vertical distance from the finished floor level at the bottom of the flight to the finished floor level at the top. The total going is the overall horizontal distance of travel from the nosing of the bottom step to the nosing of the upper floor or landing. Other items to check are the length and width of the opening in the floor, the position of the doorways either end of the stairs and finally the floor level (see Figure 2.32).

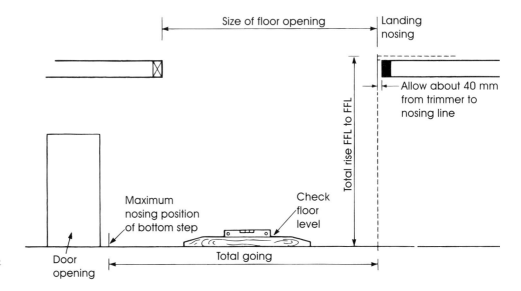

Figure 2.32
Site measurement for stairs

Other details – internal openings, and areas or recesses for screens, partitions or fitments are measured in the same way as external openings.

Depending on the nature of the survey, service details such as outlets, sockets and switches for gas, water, electricity, television, telephone, etc., may be shown, although these are often recorded on separate service plans to avoid overloading and confusing the main floor plans.

Using notes – in addition, when undertaking surveys for refurbishment purposes, brief notes should be taken, recording details of structural defects and signs of decay and deterioration. This may entail lifting several floorboards and the partial removal of panelling or casings.

Scale drawings – on returning to the workshop or office, the sketches can be drawn up to produce a set of scale drawings and any brief notes used to form the basis of the survey report. It is at this stage that the necessity of taking all the dimensions and details is realised. One vital missing dimension can be costly, as it will result in a further visit to the building at a later stage to take the dimension.

Workshop rods

Before making anything but the most simple, one-off item of joinery, it is normal practice to set out a workshop rod. This is done by the **setter-out** who translates the architect's scale details, specification and their own survey details into full-size vertical and horizontal sections of the item. In addition, particularly where shaped work is concerned, elevations may also be required. Rods are usually drawn on either thin board, thin plywood, white-painted hardboard or rolls of decorator's lining paper.

When the job with which they are concerned is complete and they are no longer required for reference, boards may be planed or sanded off and used again. Plywood and hardboard rods may be painted over with white emulsion.

Sizing – although paper rods are often considered more convenient, because of their ease in handling and storage, they are less accurate in their use. This is because paper is more susceptible to dimension changes as a result of humidity and also changes due to the inevitable creasing and folding of the paper. In order to avoid mistakes, the critical dimensions shown in Figure 2.33 should be included where paper rods are used. Sight size is the dimension between the innermost edges of the components, also known as daylight size as this is the height and width of a glazed opening which admits light. Shoulder size is the length of the member (rail or muntin) between shoulders of tenons. Overall size (O/A) is the extreme length or width of an item.

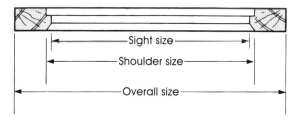

Figure 2.33
Critical dimensions

Where figured dimensions are different from the rod, always work to the stated size.

Rodding windows and doors

A typical rod for a casement window is shown in Figure 2.34. The drawings on the rod show the sections and positions of the various window components on a height and width rod. All of the component parts of the window can then be marked accurately from the rod. The rod should also contain the following information:

◆ rod number;
◆ date drawn;
◆ contract number and location;
◆ the scale drawing from which the rod was produced;
◆ the number of jobs required.

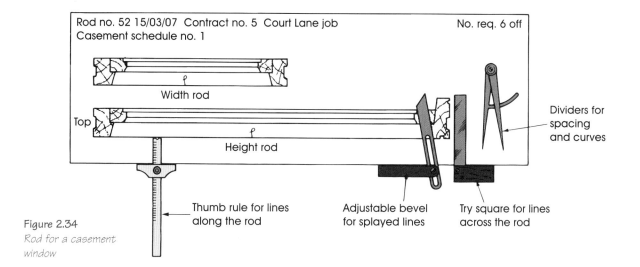

Figure 2.34
Rod for a casement window

The drawing equipment the setter-out will use to produce the rod is also shown in Figure 2.34.

◆ A thumb rule for lines along the rod.
◆ An adjustable bevel for splayed lines.
◆ A try square for lines across the rod.
◆ Dividers for spacing and curves.

It is standard practice to set out the height rod first, keeping the head or top of the item on the left of the rod and the face of the item nearest the setter-out. The width rod is drawn above the height rod, keeping identical sections in line as illustrated in Fig 2.35.

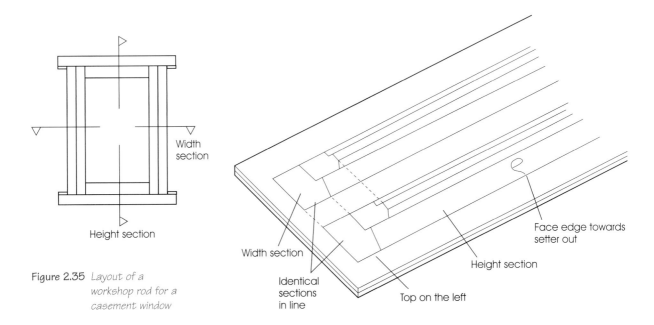

Figure 2.35 *Layout of a workshop rod for a casement window*

Illustrated in Figure 2.36 is a workshop rod for a framed, ledged and braced door. In this rod the position of the mortises have been indicated by crosses, as is the practice in many workshops. The rear elevation has also been included for the joiner's information when fitting the braces.

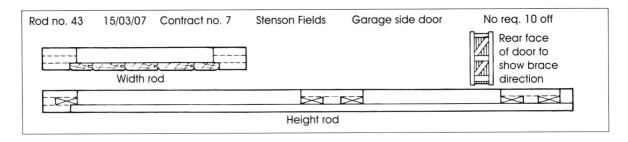

Figure 2.36 *Rod for framed, ledged and braced door*

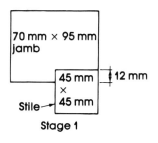

70 mm × 95 mm jamb

45 mm × 45 mm | 12 mm

Stile

Stage 1

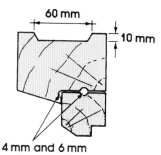

10 mm

$\frac{1}{3}$ $\frac{1}{3}$ $\frac{1}{3}$

Stage 2

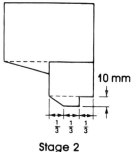

60 mm

10 mm

4 mm and 6 mm anti-capillary grooves

Stage 3

Figure 2.37 *Building up a drawing*

Preparation stages – Figure 2.37 shows the three easy stages, which can be used to build up a detailed section. This method can be used when producing both workshop rods and scale drawings:

◆ stage 1: the components are drawn in there rectangular sections;
◆ stage 2: the square and rectangular sections are added;
◆ stage 3: all other details are then added, including hatching.

It is good practice to keep the square and moulded sections the same depth. This eases the fitting of the joint, as the shoulders will be in the same position.

Sometimes it is not practical to set out the full height or width of very large items. In such cases the section may be reduced by broken lines and inserting an add-on dimension between them for use when marking out as shown in Figure 2.38.

Preparation for openings – when determining details for doors and windows the setter-out must take into account their opening radius. A number of applicable door and window sections are illustrated in Figure 2.39.

◆ Detail A shows that the closing edge must have a leading edge (bevelled off) to prevent jamming on the frame when opened.
◆ Detail B applies to the use of parliament and easy-clean hinges, which both have extended pivot points. Here, both the opening edge and frame jamb have been bevelled off at 90° to a line drawn between the pivot point and the opposite inner closing edge.
◆ Detail C shows how splayed rebates are determined for narrow double doors, bar doors and wicket gates, etc.

Figure 2.38 *Add-on dimensioning*

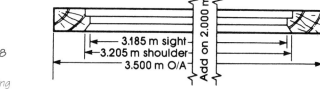

3.185 m sight
3.205 m shoulder
3.500 m O/A
Add on 2.000 m

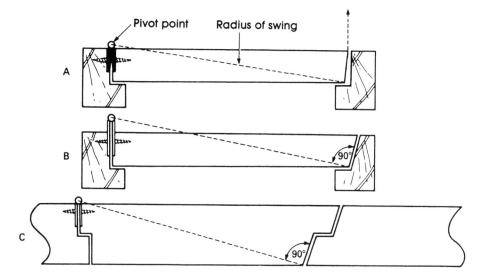

Pivot point   Radius of swing

A

B   90°

C   90°

Figure 2.39 *Opening details (doors and windows)*

Setting out for Joinery **Chapter 2**

Illustrated in Figure 2.40 is a workshop rod for a half-glazed door with diminished stiles and a shaped top rail. As the stiles section is different above and below the middle rail, two width rods are required. Also included on the rod is a half elevation of the curved top rail as its shape is not apparent from the sections.

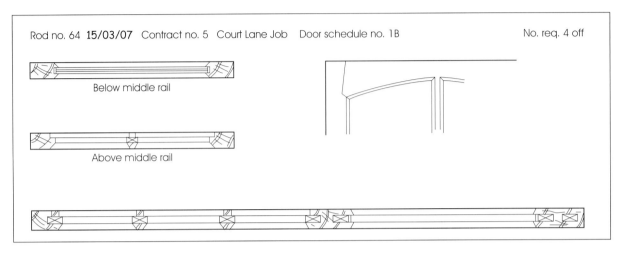

Figure 2.40 *Rod for half-glazed doors*

Rodding tables and cabinets

Rods for three-dimensional joinery items such as tables and cabinets are drawn using broken details and add-on dimensions for one or more of the sections. This is in order to represent their three, often considerable, framed dimensions on a narrow rod.

Figure 2.41 illustrates a rod for a dining table. The length and height sections are shown in full along the rod, with the full width section being positioned under the length.

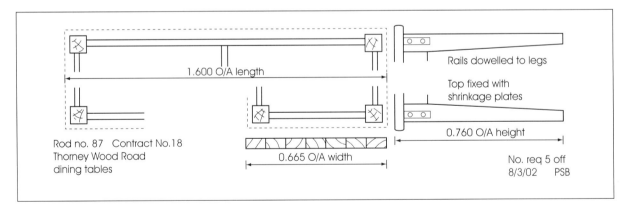

Figure 2.41 *Rod for three-dimensional item (dining table)*

Figure 2.42 illustrates a rod for a cabinet (floor unit), to be constructed from melamine-faced chipboard (MFC) with hardwood trims. A circled detail (not part of the rod) shows that the carcass is rebated out and screwed together. The hardwood trims are glued and pinned in position after assembly to conceal the screw fixings. Also included on this rod are notes on assembly for use by the marker-out and joiners.

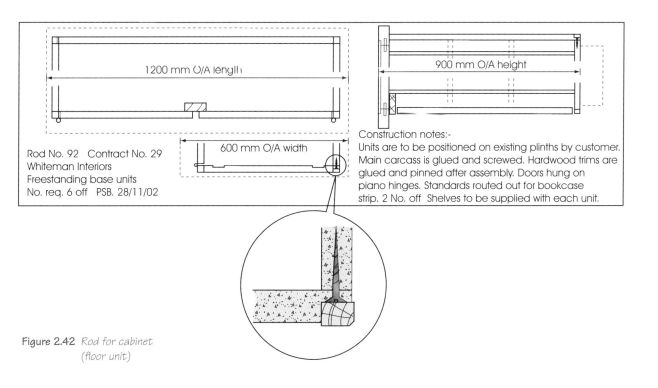

1200 mm O/A length

900 mm O/A height

600 mm O/A width

Rod No. 92   Contract No. 29
Whiteman Interiors
Freestanding base units
No. req. 6 off   PSB. 28/11/02

Construction notes:-
Units are to be positioned on existing plinths by customer. Main carcass is glued and screwed. Hardwood trims are glued and pinned after assembly. Doors hung on piano hinges. Standards routed out for bookcase strip. 2 No. off Shelves to be supplied with each unit.

Figure 2.42 *Rod for cabinet (floor unit)*

Rodding stairs

Rods for stairs are often drawn showing the top and bottom details, with the width section positioned between them. See Figure 2.43.

Where newels form part of the construction these should be drawn to show the housings for the treads and risers, and mortises for the string. To accompany these details the setter-out should supply storey and going rods on timber battens, as shown in Figure 2.44. These are set out using the total rise and going of the stair taken during the site survey. Further information is not required as the marker-out will make a set of templates from these details in order to complete the task.

Before setting out storey and going rods for a flight of stairs, it is necessary to determine the individual rise and going for each step.

♦ The rise of each step is determined by dividing the total rise (vertical measurement from finished floor to finished floor) by the number of risers required.
♦ The going of each step is determined by dividing the total going (horizontal measurement from bottom step nosing to landing nosing) by the number of treads required (one less than the number of risers).

These dimensions are controlled by the Building Regulations. Chapter 4, on the manufacture of joinery products, contains details for typical situations.

did you know?

The rise and going of steps and thus pitch of stairs is controlled by Building Regulations. Refer to ADK: Protection from falling, collision and impact.

Setting out for Joinery **Chapter 2**

Chapter 2 Setting out for Joinery

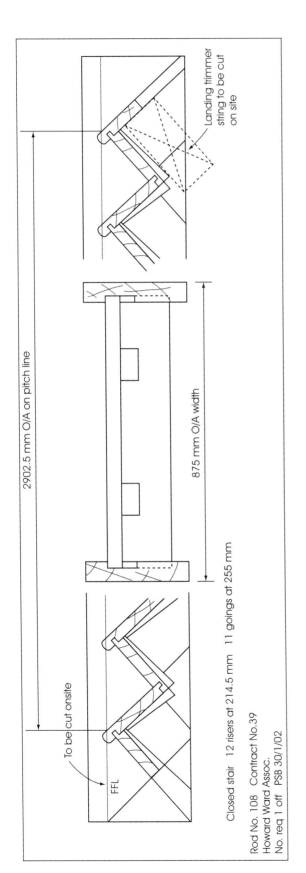

Landing trimmer string to be cut on site

To be cut onsite

FFL

2902.5 mm O/A on pitch line

875 mm O/A width

Closed stair 12 risers at 214.5 mm 11 goings at 255 mm

Rod No. 108   Contract No.39
Howard Ward Assoc.
No. req 1 off   PSB 30/1/02

Figure 2.43 Rod for a closed stair (no newels)

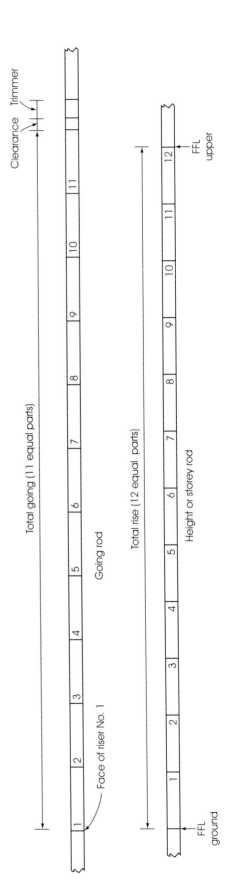

Clearance   Trimmer

Total going (11 equal parts)

Going rod

Face of riser No. 1

Total rise (12 equal parts)

Height or storey rod

FFL upper

FFL ground

Figure 2.44 Storey and going rods

example

Internal flight for a dwelling house with a total rise of 2574 mm and a restricted going of 2805 mm, assuming that the minimum number of steps are required:

♦ Minimum number of risers = total rise ÷ maximum permitted rise for location of stair (220 mm in this case) = 2574 mm ÷ 220 mm = 11.7, say 12 (each measuring less than the maximum permitted).

♦ Individual rise = total rise ÷ number of risers = 2574 mm ÷ 12 = 214.5 mm.

♦ Individual going = total going ÷ number of treads (always one less than the number of risers) = 2805 mm ÷ 11 = 255 mm.

♦ Maximum pitch (in this case) = 42°. Draw rise and going full size and check the angle with a protractor, see below. In this case it measures 40°, which is permissible.

Where the pitch measures greater than 42° it can be reduced by introducing an extra rise and going, thereby slackening the pitch. However, this will increase the total going, so that stairs with restricted goings (such as those with a doorway at the bottom of the stairs) will require a total redesign in order to comply, possibly by the introduction of a landing to change the direction on the plan.

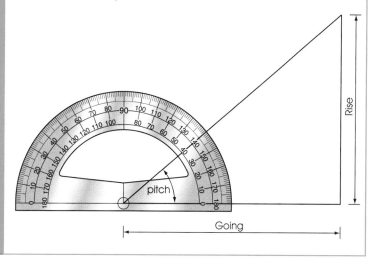

Cutting lists

When the rod has been completed the setter-out will prepare a cutting list of all material required for the job. The list will accompany the rod throughout the manufacturing operations. It is used by the machinists to select and prepare the required materials with the minimum amount of waste. The cutting list or a duplicate copy will finally be passed on to the office for job costing purposes.

There is no standard layout for cutting lists as their format varies between firms. However, it is important that they contain the following information as a minimum:

♦ details of the job, job title or description, date, rod and contract number;
♦ description of each item;
♦ quantity of each item required (no. off);
♦ finished size of each item.

A typical cutting list for six casement windows is shown in Figure 2.45. The length of each item shown on the cutting list should be the precise length to be cut. It must include an allowance over the lengths shown on the rod for manufacturing purposes.

Cutting list		
Rod no. 52	Date	Contact no. 5
Job title	Casement window	
Item	No. off	Finished size (mm)
Frame:		
Jambs	12	70×95×1000
Head	6	70×95×700
Sill	6	70×120×700
Casement:		
Stiles	12	45×45×900
Top rail	6	45×45×500
Bottom rail	6	45×70×500

Figure 2.45 *Cutting list*

◆ Between 50mm and 75mm is the normal allowance for each horn on heads and sills, to take the thrust of wedging up and to allow for 'building in'.
◆ A horn of at least 25mm is required at each end of stiles for both wedging and protection purposes.
◆ An allowance of at least 10mm in length is made for rails that are to be wedged.

An alternative more detailed cutting list for the same six casement windows is illustrated in Figure 2.46. In addition to the previous cutting list, it also includes the following:

◆ an item number that can be crayoned on each piece to allow its easy identification during all stages of manufacture;
◆ the sawn sectional sizes of the items to simplify the timber selection, machining and final costing of the job;
◆ the type of material to be used for each item, e.g. softwood, hardwood or sheet material, etc.

Figure 2.46 *Detailed cutting list*

Cutting list					
Rod no. 52		Date		Contract no. 5	
Job title		Casement window			
Item no.	Item	No. off	Finished size (mm)	Sawn size	Material
	Frame:				
1	Jambs	12	70×95×1000	75×100×1000	Redwood
2	Head	6	70×95×700	75×100×700	Redwood
3	Sill	6	70×120×700	75×125×700	Oak
	Casement:				
4	Stiles	12	45×45×500	50×50×500	Redwood
5	Top rail	6	45×45×900	50×50×900	Redwood
6	Bottom rail	6	45×70×500	50×75×500	Redwood

Computer-aided setting out

Many medium to large joinery firms now utilise computers as an aid to producing workshop rods. Setters-out input the job details into a CAD (computer-aided design) software programme, to produce both scale and full size drawings/rods. These can be printed out on a plotter for workshop use. The use of CAD in this way has the added advantage for specifying future jobs. Standard details can be stored in the computer for a range of commonly produced joinery items, requiring only dimensions to be added/adjusted in order to customise the rod before printing out for each new job.

Illustrated in Figure 2.47 is a typical joinery shop standard data sheet for an external glazed door. The computer software has been developed so that on inputting the required sizes, the rod will automatically be adjusted to suit and can then be printed off on the plotter. The computer can also be programmed to produce cutting lists at the same time.

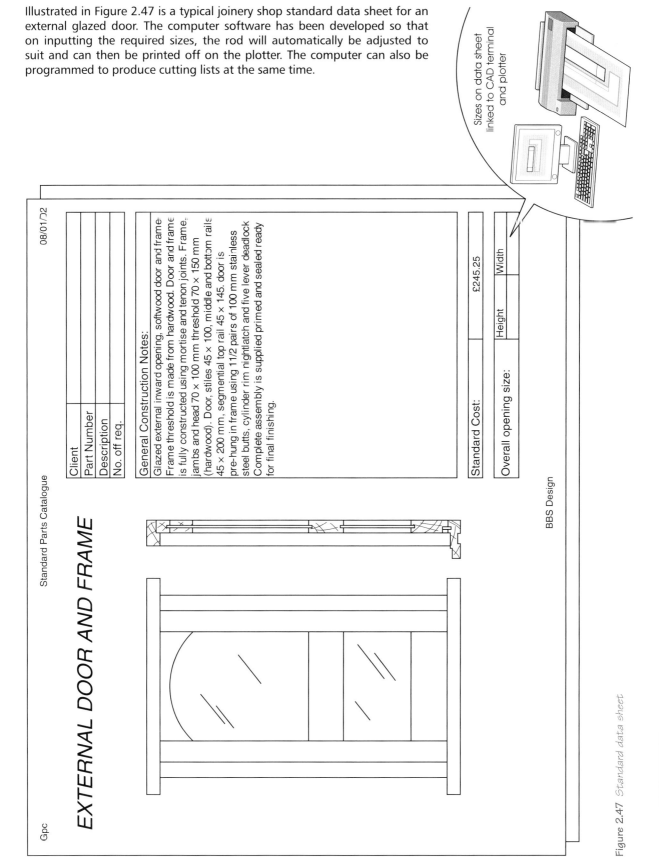

Sizes on data sheet linked to CAD terminal and plotter

Standard Parts Catalogue

08/01/02

Gpc

EXTERNAL DOOR AND FRAME

Client	
Part Number	
Description	
No. off req.	

General Construction Notes:

Glazed external inward opening, softwood door and frame. Frame threshold is made from hardwood. Door and frame is fully constructed using mortise and tenon joints. Frame jambs and head 70 × 100 mm threshold 70 × 150 mm (hardwood). Door, stiles 45 × 100, middle and bottom rails 45 × 200 mm, segmental top rail 45 × 145, door is pre-hung in frame using 11/2 pairs of 100 mm stainless steel butts, cylinder rim nightlatch and five lever deadlock. Complete assembly is supplied primed and sealed ready for final finishing.

Standard Cost:	£245.25

Overall opening size:		
	Height	Width

BBS Design

Figure 2.47 *Standard data sheet*

Setting out for Joinery **Chapter 2**

The outline elevation and cutting list for a casement window showing finished sizes is illustrated in Figure 2.48.

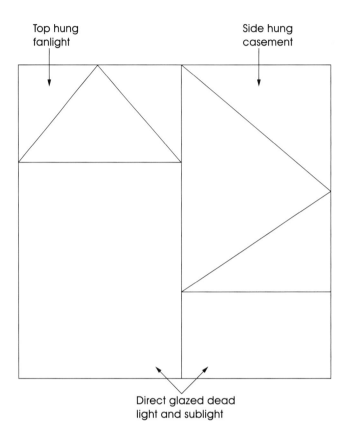

Cutting list					
Rod no.		Date		Contact no.	
Job title		Casement window			
Item no.	Item	No. off	Finished size (mm)	Sawn size	Material
	Frame:				
1	Jambs		70×95×1220		Redwood
2	Head		70×95×1350		Redwood
3	Sill		70×95×1350		Redwood
4	Transoms		70×95×600		Redwood
	Casement:				
5	Stiles		45×45×900		Redwood
6	Top rail		45×45×550		Redwood
7	Bottom rail		45×70×550		Redwood
	Fanlight:				
8	Stiles		45×45×300		Redwood
9	Top rail		45×45×550		Redwood
10	Bottom rail		45×70×550		Redwood

Figure 2.48 *Outline elevation and cutting list for a caement window*

Copy the table then complete the columns to show the material requirements for a batch of 12. Allow 5 mm for planing on each section size when entering the sawn sizes.

Using the sawn sizes, calculate the total cost of material required for the batch of twelve, if the cost of US softwood is £235.52 per m³. Add cutting and wastage allowance of 20%.

You have determined a target time of 2.25 hours for manufacturing each window. Calculate the total time required to manufacture the batch of twelve, including an addition of 15% for planning and contingencies.

Determine the total cost of materials and labour for the batch of 12 to be charged to the customer, if the company's labour charge-out rate is £15.65 per hour and 35% is added to both material costs and labour rates for overheads and profit.

Total cost of material =

Total time to manufacture =

Selling price =

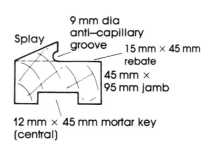

Splay
9 mm dia anti-capillary groove
15 mm × 45 mm rebate
45 mm × 95 mm jamb
12 mm × 45 mm mortar key (central)

Figure 2.49 *Jamb of a door frame*

Draw full size the jamb of a door frame shown in Figure 2.49. (Draw the rectangular sections first, then add the details.) Add lines to the above section to show the door frame head. Indicate the mortise position.

1. Explain the reason why workshop rods are drawn full size and not to scale.

2. Produce a sketch to show the difference between the sight size, shoulder size and overall size of a joinery product.

3. State the maximum width of a 15 mm thick tenon.

4. List five items of information that can be obtained from a setting-out rod.

5. (a) Define the term 'weathering'; (b) state the purpose of including 'weathering' in an item of joinery.

6. A cross is used on a timber section shown on a workshop rod to denote a: (a) tenon, (b) mortise, (c) rebate (d) groove.

7. Describe a circumstance where add-on dimensions may be used on a rod.

8. Calculate the individual rise of a step for a staircase that has 14 risers and a total rise of 2740 mm.

9. Setting out details may be produced using a CAD system. Define what this abbreviation means.

10. Explain why it is good practice to keep square and moulded sections the same depth when designing joinery items.

Marking Out for Joinery

This chapter is intended to provide the reader with an overview of marking out for joinery work. Its contents are assessed in the NVQ Unit VR 15 Mark Out from Setting Out Details for Routine Products.

In this chapter you will cover the following range of topics:

- ◆ manufacturing operations;
- ◆ timber selection;
- ◆ marking out framed joinery;
- ◆ marking out three-dimensional joinery;
- ◆ methods, briefings and costing.

What is required in VR 15?

To successfully complete this unit you will be required to demonstrate your skill and knowledge of the following marking-out processes:

- ◆ interpreting information;
- ◆ adopting safe and healthy working practices;
- ◆ selecting materials, components and equipment;
- ◆ marking out details for internal and external joinery products.

You will be required practically to:

- ◆ mark out from setting out details and cutting lists, for a range of joinery products including:
  - ► doors
  - ► frames (glazed and non-glazed)
  - ► linings
  - ► units and/or fitments
  - ► staircases;
- ◆ proportion joints;
- ◆ use marking and testing tools;
- ◆ take workplace dimensions;
- ◆ communicate with other team members, including machinists and joiners;
- ◆ undertake calculations for quantity, measurement or costs;
- ◆ requisition materials.

Definitions

Marking out – referring to design drawings, workshop rods and cutting lists produced during the setting-out process, the selection and marking out of timbers, to show the exact position of joints, mouldings, sections and shapes. In addition may also include the making of jigs for later manufacturing or assembly operations.

Manufacturing operations – the basic operations that are undertaken during the small to medium scale production of joinery items, follow the traditional sequence of working by hand. However, machinists undertake most of the work, with the joiner only being involved at assembly. These operations are briefly described in Table 3.1. They are listed in workshop sequence and apply to traditional solid timber, framed joinery manufacture. Typical machines for the smaller joinery works are listed. Larger works will have additional or alternative machines, such as a multi-head planer and moulder; a double-ended tenoning machine; or even CNC (computer numerical control) machines.

Table 3.1 *Typical sequence of operations for a small joinery works*

Operation	Description	Typical machine used
1. Setting out	The translation of design drawings and specification into production drawings, rods and cutting lists.	
2. Cross cutting	The selection and cutting to length of timber shown on the cutting list.	Pull over cross-cut saw
3. Ripping	The cutting of listed timber to its sawn or 'nominal' width and thickness.	Circular rip saw bench
4. Surface planning	The accurate preparation of the face side and edge.	Surface planer or combination planer
5. Thicknessing	The preparation and reduction in size of the material to the required width and thickness.	Panel planer or combination planer
6. Marking out	The selection and marking out of timbers, to show the exact position of joints, mouldings, sections and shapes.	
7. Mortising	The cutting of mortises and haunches.	Chisel or chain mortiser
8. Tenoning	The cutting of tenons to suit mortises and the production of scribed shoulders.	Single-ended tenoner
9. Moulding	The running of mouldings and other sections.	Spindle moulder
10. Assembly	The fitting of joints, gluing, cramping, squaring and final cleaning up of an item of joinery.	

Timber selection

Radial-sawn sections are normally preferred for joinery as these remain fairly stable, with little tendency to shrink or distort (see Figure 3.1). However, for clear finished work this factor may take second place, as the important consideration will then be which face of a particular timber is the most decorative; for example as illustrated in Figure 3.2:

- radial face oak gives figured or silver grain;
- tangential face Douglas fir gives flame figuring.

Grain

The timber's grain and defects must also be considered when marking out and machining. Careful positioning of a **face mark** (the leg of the mark points

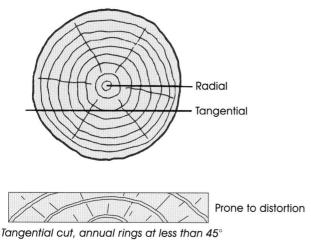

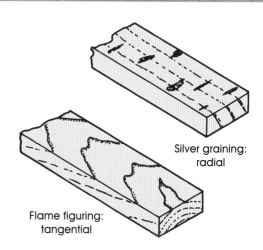

Radial

Tangential

Silver graining:
radial

Prone to distortion

Tangential cut, annual rings at less than 45°

Flame figuring:
tangential

Fairly stable

Radial cut, annual rings at 45° or more

Figure 3.2 *Figuring*

Figure 3.1 *Timber conversion*

did you know?

Face marks look like a '9' with the leg pointing towards the face edge. Face edge marks are an open arrowhead or inverted 'V' with its point joining up with the face side mark.

towards the face edge) may allow defects such as knots, pith and wane, etc. to be machined out later by a rebate or a moulding as shown in Figure 3.3. Knots and short graining should be avoided, especially near joints or on mouldings.

Grain direction must be considered also when marking up faces, in anticipation of later machining operations. For the best finish, diagonal grain should slope into the cutter rotation as shown in Figure 3.4. The grain will tend to break out if marked the other way.

The visual effect of grain direction and colour shading for painted work is of little importance, but careful consideration is required for hardwood and other clear-finished joinery.

Marking out for Joinery

Chapter 3

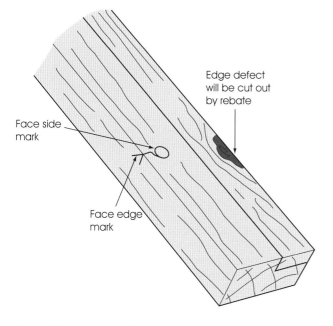

Face side
mark

Edge defect
will be cut out
by rebate

Face edge
mark

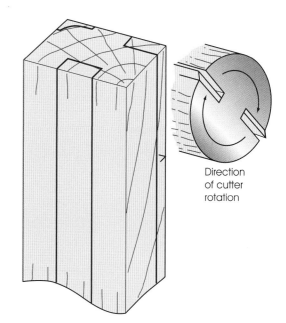

Direction
of cutter
rotation

Figure 3.3 *Positioning of face mark*

Figure 3.4 *Grain direction and cutter rotation*

Decorative matching

The aim is to produce a decorative and well-balanced effect. Figure 3.5 illustrates a pair of well-matched panel doors. The meeting stiles have been cut from one board so that their grain matches. Likewise, adjacent rails have been cut from one continuous board to provide a continuity of grain. Any heavily grained or darker shaded timber is best kept to the bottom of an item for an impression of balance and stability. If these were placed at the top, the item would appear to be 'top-heavy'. Panels should be matched and have their arched top grain features pointing upwards (see Figure 3.6).

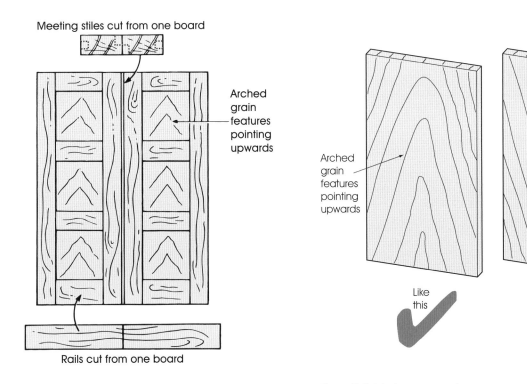

Meeting stiles cut from one board

Arched grain features pointing upwards

Arched grain features pointing upwards

Rails cut from one board

Like this

Not like this

Figure 3.5 *Grain matching*

Figure 3.6 *Marking out panels*

did you know?

Radially sliced veneers may be called quarter-cut veneers and tangentially sliced veneers showing 'arched grain' feature as 'crown cut' veneers.

Edge jointed members are best matched by deeping a thicker section and opening out, just as the pages of this book are opened, as shown in Figure 3.7. This method of timber matching is termed 'book matching'. Where this is not possible, different boards should be positioned edge-to-edge to obtain the best match, and marked up for machining. See Figure 3.8.

Veneers

Plywoods are mostly manufactured using rotary cut veneers, which produce a widely varying grain pattern that is not usually considered very decorative. Therefore, when plywoods and other veneered sheet materials are used for clear finished work their surface should be veneered with a radially or tangentially sliced veneer. See Figure 3.9. When hand veneering for table tops and panels, etc., there are a number of different ways in which veneers may be matched in order to create different decorative effects. A number of typical matching arrangements are illustrated in Figure 3.10.

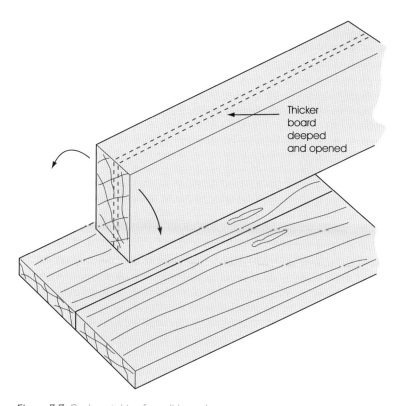

Thicker
board
deeped
and opened

Figure 3.7 *Book matching for solid panels*

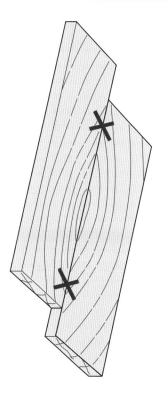

Figure 3.8 *Grain matched and marked for jointing*

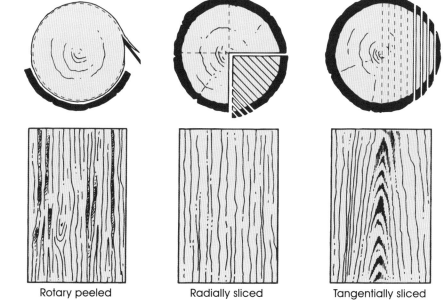

Rotary peeled   Radially sliced   Tangentially sliced

Figure 3.9 *Veneer cutting*

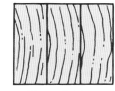

Figure 3.10 *Veneer matching*   Book matching   Quarter matching   Slip matching

Marking out

After the timber has been prepared and faces marked, the actual marking out of the item can be undertaken. Depending on the size of the joinery works and the volume of work it handles, setting out and marking out may either be undertaken by one person or treated as separate roles to be undertaken by different people.

Framed joinery

A workshop rod for a glazed door is illustrated in Figure 3.11. It shows how a stile and rail are laid on the rod; the sight, shoulder and mortise position lines are squared up with the aid of a set square. The mortises, tenons and sections, etc., are marked out as shown in the completed stile, Figure 3.12. Most details are simply pencilled on, however mortises should be marked with gauge lines and the shoulders of tenons marked with a marking knife.

In many joiners' shops it is standard practice to sketch the section on a member to enable all who handle it to see instantly how it should look when finished. The marked-out member is also marked up with the rod or job number, so that it may be identified with the rod/job, throughout manufacturing operations.

Where a paired or handed member is required (stiles and jambs) the two pieces can be placed together on a bench with their face sides apart, as all squaring should be done from the face side or edge for accuracy. The lines can then be squared over onto the second piece as shown in Figure 3.13. When pre-sectioned timber has to be marked out, a box square, as shown in Figure 3.14, can be used to transfer the lines around the section.

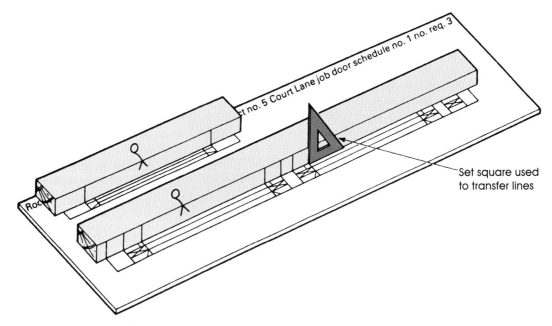

Figure 3.11 *Marking out from rod*

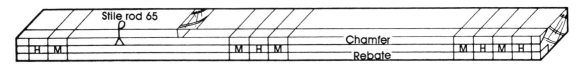

Figure 3.12 *Marked-out stile*

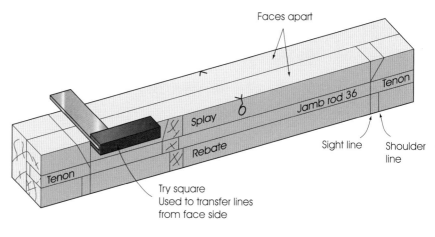

Faces apart

Splay

Rebate

Jamb rod 36

Tenon

Tenon

Sight line

Shoulder line

Try square
Used to transfer lines
from face side

Figure 3.13 *Transferring marks to the second of a pair*

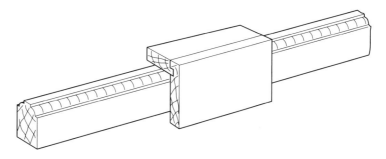

Figure 3.14 *Use of a box square*

Using a pattern

did you know?

For accuracy, marking out
should be done from the
face side or face edge only.

Whenever more than one joinery item of a particular design is required, the first to be marked out becomes a pattern for the rest of the job. After checking the patterns against the rod for accuracy, they can be used to mark out all other pieces, and set up the machines. The positions of the mortises are normally marked out on every member, as it is not economical to spend time setting up chisel or chain mortising machines to work to stops, except where very long runs are concerned. Shoulder lines for tenons are required on the pattern only, as tenoning machines are easily set up to stops enabling all similar members with tenons in a batch to be accurately machined to one setting.

Information for the machinist should be included on the pattern, as to how many or how many pairs are required. Figure 3.15 illustrates the pattern head and jamb for a batch of 10 door frames.

Figure 3.16 shows a pattern being used to mark out a batch of paired stiles. As any distortion of the timber could result in inaccuracies, they must be firmly cramped together.

The use of this method ensures greater accuracy than if each piece were to be individually marked from the rod. Alternatively, a batch of stiles can be cramped between two patterns and the positions marked across with the aid of a short, straight edge. At the end of a run the patterns can be machined, fitted and assembled to produce the final item.

Marking out for Joinery

Chapter 3

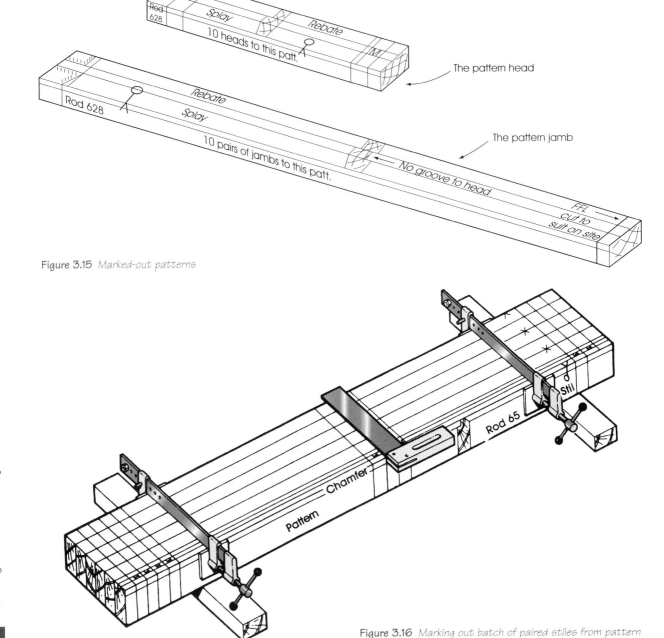

Figure 3.15 *Marked-out patterns*

Figure 3.16 *Marking out batch of paired stiles from pattern*

Three-dimensional joinery

did you know?

Jigs and templates save time when marking out and working large batches.

Marking out for three-dimensional items follows the methods used for framed joinery, each component part having its own individual pattern containing information for the machinist. Where sheet material is concerned this may be marked out on the actual component part or a thin plywood or MDF template/ jig may be produced. Illustrated in Figure 3.17 is the design drawing for a base unit, a data sheet for one of its standards and a plywood template marked up and drilled out, to be used as a machining jig.

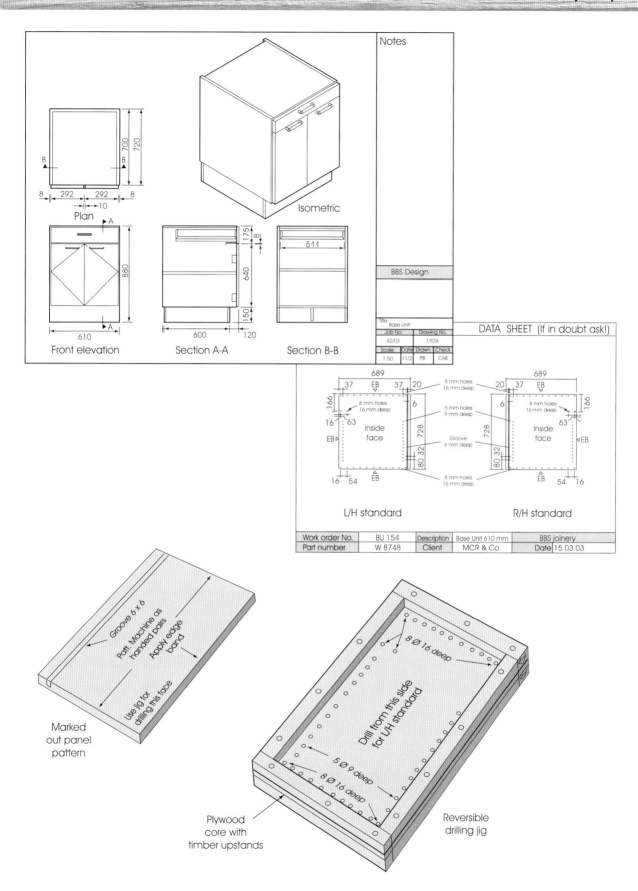

Figure 3.17 *Base unit details*

Joinery works with computer-controlled boring or routing facilities will programme the machines directly from the data sheet, without any need to mark out panels or make templates.

Stairs

The marker-out will make a number of templates out of thin plywood or MDF to assist in the marking out of stairs. See Figure 3.18.

Pitchboard is an accurately prepared right-angled triangle with its two shorter sides conforming precisely to the individual rise and going dimensions of those on the rods.

Margin template is made as a tee piece, with its projection equal to the distance above the tread and riser intersection to the upper edge of the string.

Combined pitch and margin template may be made as an alternative and is often preferred for ease of use.

Tread and riser templates are equal to the shape of the tread and riser plus the allowance for wedging. It is good practice to make the slope for the wedge the same on both templates, so that only one type of wedge needs to be used when the stairs are assembled.

Marking out strings

These are marked out as a left and right handed pair for closed stairs, or as a handed wall and open string for stairs open on one side. See Figure 3.19.

Marking out for Joinery

Chapter 3

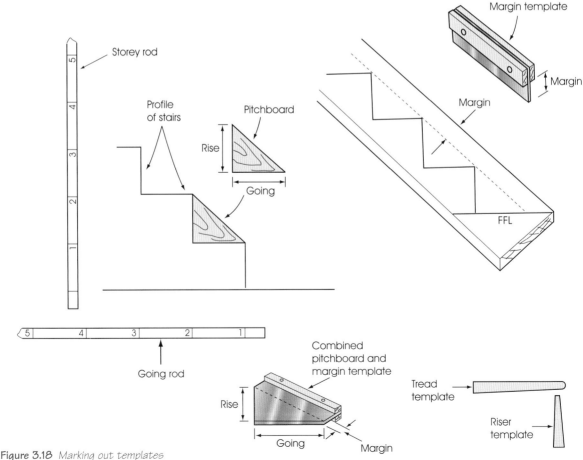

Figure 3.18 *Marking out templates*

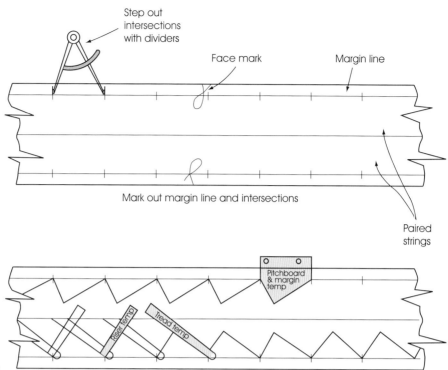

Step out intersections with dividers

Face mark

Margin line

Mark out margin line and intersections

Paired strings

Pitchboard & margin temp

Riser temp

Tread temp

Figure 3.19 *Marking out strings for housing*

Use templates to mark out step profiles and housings

- Mark face side and edge on machined timber. Place paired strings on the bench, face sides up and face edges apart.
- Pencil on pitch or margin line on strings, using either margin template or adjustable square.
- Set pair of dividers to hypotenuse (longest side) of pitchboard and step out along the margin line. This establishes the tread and riser intersection points. It is good practice to step out the intersections rather than just rely on the pitchboard, as each step could progressively grow by the thickness of the pencil line.
- Line up pitchboard and margin template on each stepped-out position in turn and pencil on the rise and going of each step.
- Using the tread and riser templates, pencil their housing positions on to the strings. It is normal practice to leave the ends of strings long and square for cutting to suit on site. The outer string for an open-side stair will require marking out at both ends for tenons. See Figure 3.20.
- Mark out tenon at bottom of stair. A bull-nosed step is being used in this case. The face of the second riser in this case is taken to be the centre line of the newel. Measure at a right-angle to the riser, half the newel thickness. Mark a plumb line using the riser edge of the pitchboard. This will give the shoulder line of the tenon. On occasions the shoulder is recessed into the newel face by about 5 mm to conceal shrinkage; if this is the case the shoulder will require extending forwards to allow for it. Alternatively a barefaced tenon may be specified to conceal shrinkage on one face.
- Repeat the previous stage at the top end of the string, except this time the centre line of the newel will be the face of the top riser.
- From the shoulder line measure at a right angle again, three-quarters of the newel thickness, to give the tenon length. Divide the tenon as shown to give a twin tenon with a central haunch. The bottom end of the string will have an additional haunch at its lower edge, whilst the upper part of the tenon at the top end of the string will be cut off level. This arrangement of tenons is to avoid undercutting the mortises or weakness caused by short grain, if other arrangements are used.

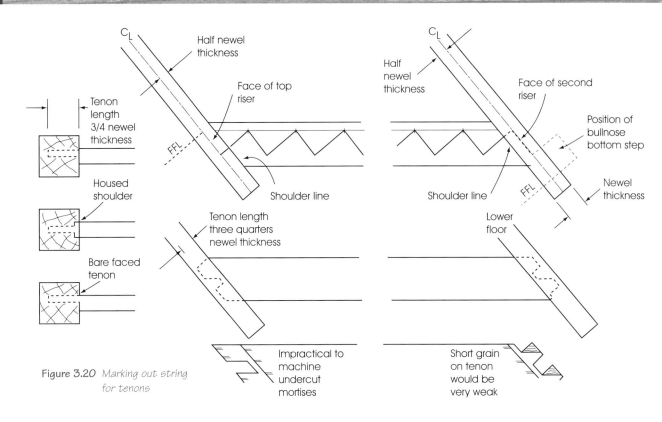

Figure 3.20 *Marking out string for tenons*

did you know?

Heights of handrails on stairs and landings as well as balustrades are controlled by the Building Regulations. See ADK: Protection from falling, collision and impact. Remember you can consult this online at www.planning portal.gov.uk.

Marking out newels

The marking out is illustrated in Figure 3.21. The four faces of the newel are drawn out to show the housing and mortise positions. The upper edges of both newels will also require mortising to receive the handrail.

Marking out handrail and balustrade

The overall height of the handrail on the stairs is 900 mm above the pitch line. On upper landings this is either 900 mm or 1000 mm above the floor level, depending on the use of the building. See Figure 3.22.

- ◆ Handrails are normally tenoned into the mortised newels. The shoulder angle and line of the handrail tenons (and capping if used) will be the same as the string. Balusters may be either stub tenoned into the edge of the string, or fitted in a groove run into a string capping, which itself is grooved over the string. At their upper end they are normally pinned into the groove run on the underside of the handrail, or again they may be stub tenoned. Distance pieces may be cut between balusters and pinned into the grooves to maintain the baluster spacings.
- ◆ Determine the number of balusters required. Allow two per tread and one where there is a newel. For an 11-going flight with a bottom bullnose step there will be eight full treads and two part treads between newels, thus 18 balusters will be required.
- ◆ Determine the horizontal distance between balusters. Divide the horizontal distance between the newels (less space taken up by total width of all balusters) by the number of balusters plus one. There will always be one more space than the number of balusters.

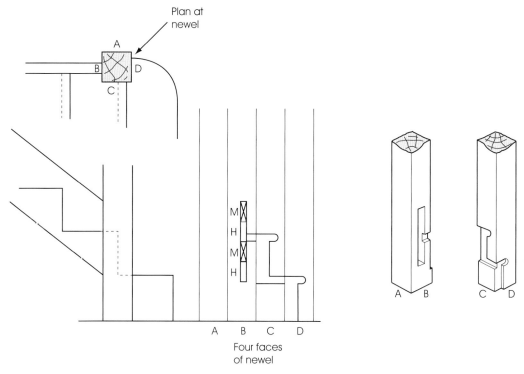

Figure 3.21 *Marking out newels*

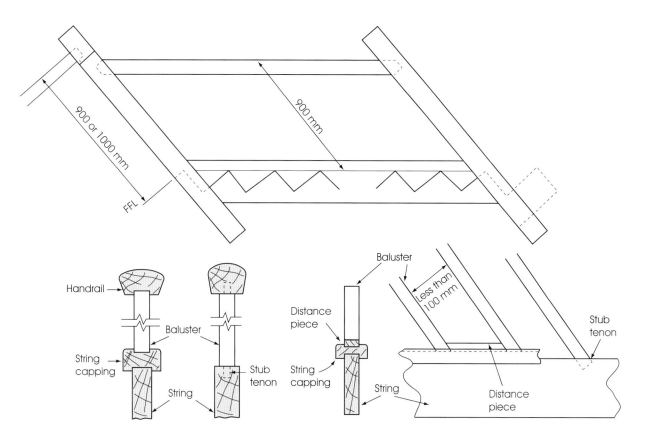

Figure 3.22 *Marking out for handrail and balustrade*

Distance between newels = 10 treads x going – newel width

= (10 × 255) – 100

= 2450 mm

Space taken by balusters = number of balusters × width

= 18 × 40

= 720 mm

Distance between balusters = Distance between newels – space taken by balusters ÷ number of balusters + 1

$$= \frac{2450 - 720}{19}$$

= 91 mm

The maximum distance between balusters should be such that a 100 mm sphere (less than a small child's head) is not able to pass between them. At 91 mm this example is acceptable for straight balusters. However, if turned balusters were to be used the space between the turned sections may exceed 100 mm. If this were the case an additional baluster should be added and the distance between recalculated.

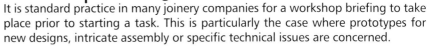

Methods, briefings and costings

Method statement

At some stage in the setting and marking-out process, a method statement is often produced. This sets out the main operations that have to be undertaken in order to complete a specific task. Figure 3.23 illustrates a typical joinery method statement for a batch of floor units. This would be passed to the joiners for guidance prior to them starting the task.

Workshop briefing

It is standard practice in many joinery companies for a workshop briefing to take place prior to starting a task. This is particularly the case where prototypes for new designs, intricate assembly or specific technical issues are concerned.

The briefing meeting, normally held by the setter/marker-out, will often bring together the machinist and joiner to familiarise them with the task and its specific requirements. A further briefing may take place once the materials have been machined prior to assembly, to consider methods and give assembly-specific instructions.

did you know?

Briefings allow all concerned to familiarise themselves with the work in hand and to decide a common approach.

Determining costs

The setter-out/marker-out is in many organisations responsible for determining shop floor costs. This may involve both the calculation of material costs and the cost of labour.

Material costs

Material costs are determined by taking off the m³ of solid timber and m² of sheet materials required for a job from the cutting list. Plus the cost of any ironmongery (an allowance is not normally made for consumables such as glue, nails and screws, etc.).

A percentage is added to these quantities for cutting and waste, before the purchasing price of the materials is applied.

JOINERY METHOD STATEMENT

Works Order Number	15350	Del. Date	30-1-03	Part Number	BU14 MEW
Description	BASE UNIT 610 mm			Client	MEAL-E-WAY
Unit Time hrs	1·95	Quantity	10 off	Total Time hrs	19·5

No.	Operations
1	Assemble unit carcass to assembly details, using cascamite glue and dowels. Fix back of unit to base and sub top using 25 mm ring shank nails.
2	Assemble plinth using cascamite glue and plated screws. Fix to unit using 8 off white plastic modesty blocks.
3	Assemble drawer and install in unit, using bottom mounted steel runners. Fix slab front and ironmongery as detailed.
4	Hang doors and fit ironmongery as detailed.
5	Insert shelf studs and shelf.
6	Remove all arrises and wipe down all surfaces.
7	Undertake final quality check, label and transfer to pallet.
8	
9	
10	

Figure 3.23 Joinery method statement (not definitive – provided as a guide only)

example

Figure 3.24 shows a cutting list for a batch of 10 external doors and frames. Also included on the bottom of the list are the ironmongery requirements.

◆ It is company standard practice to add 50 mm to the finished component length, to allow for squaring off ends. The normal 5 mm has been allowed on the sectional size for planning.
◆ 15% is added to the m^3 quantities for cutting and waste.
◆ Use the sawn (also known as breakout) sizes to determine volume of each component.
◆ Total volume of like materials and add percentage for cutting and waste.
◆ Multiply by cost using figures below.

US redwood = £246.50 m^3

FAS oak = £695.75 m^3

100 mm stainless steel hinges = £5.90 per pair

Night latch (stainless steel case) = £28.42 each

5 lever mortise deadlock (stainless steel foreplate) = £32.40 each

6 x 25 mm stainless steel water bar = £15.90 per 3 m length

Volume of softwood:

Head	10 x 1.2 x 0.1 x 0.075	= 0.09 m^3
Jambs	20 x 2.25 x 0.1 x 0.075	= 0.3375 m^3
Top rail	10 x 0.96 x 0.15 x 0.05	= 0.072 m^3
Mid rail	10 x 0.96 x 0.225 x 0.05	= 0.108 m^3
Bottom rail	10 x 0.96 x 0.225 x 0.05	= 0.108 m^3
Stiles	20 x 2.19 x 0.1 x 0.05	= 0.219 m^3
Total volume softwood		= 0.9345 m^3
Cutting and waste allowance		= 0.9345 x 1.15
		= 1.075 m^3 (to 3 decimal places)
Total cost of softwood		= 1.075 x £246.50 = £264.99

Volume of hardwood:

Threshold	10 x 1.2 x 0.15 x 0.075	= 0.135 m^3
Cutting and waste allowance 15%		= 0.135 x 1.15
		= 0.155 m^3
Total cost of hardwood		= 0.155 x £695.75 = £107.84

Other costings:

Total cost of timber	= £264.99 + £107.84	
	= £372.83	
Cost of 30 hinges at £5.90 per pair	= 15 x £5.90	= £88.50
Cost of 10 night latches at £28.42 each	= 10 x £28.42	= £284.20
Cost of 10 deadlocks at £32.40 each	= 10 x £32.40	= £324.00
Cost of 10 x 1m lengths of water-bar at £15.90 per 3m for say 4 lengths	= 4 x £15.90	= £63.60
Total cost of ironmongery	= £88.50 + £284.20 + £324.00 + £63.60	
	= £760.30	
Total cost of materials (timber and ironmongery)	= £372.83 + £760.30	
	= £1133.13	

CUTTING LIST

For: BBS Joinery

| Client: | A. J. SIMS PLC | Part Number: | AJS 1/4 | Description: | EXTERNAL DOOR & FRAME | Date: 10-3-02 |

Component Number:	Quantity required:	Component Description:	Breakout Sizes (sawn)			Material Description:	Finished sizes:			Remarks:
			Length	Width	Thickness		Length	Width	Thickness	
EDF 1.1	10	Head	1200	100	75	US Redwood	1150	95	70	MTD
EDF 1.2	10	Threshold	1200	150	75	FAS Oak	1150	145	70	MTD
EDF 1.3	20	Jambs	2250	100	75	US Redwood	2200	95	70	MTD
EDF 1.4	10	Top rail	960	150	50	US Redwood	910	145	45	MTD
EDF 1.5	10	Middle rail	960	225	50	US Redwood	910	220	45	MTD
EDF 1.6	10	Bottom rail	960	225	50	US Redwood	910	220	45	MTD
EDF 1.7	20	Stiles	2190	100	50	US Redwood	2140	95	45	MTD
IRONMONGERY										
HSS100	30	100 mm hinge				Stainless steel				
CRNL2	10	Night latch				Stainless steel casing				
MDL4	10	Mortise deadlock				5 lever SS fore plate				
WB1	10	Water bar				Stainless steel	1000	25		6 Joiners cut to length

* MTD = Machine to detail   NFM = No further machining

Figure 3.24 Cutting list for external doors and frames

Labour costs

Labour costs are determined from the estimated length of time required to complete a task. These may be derived from:

◆ company standard times;
◆ records of past performance; or
◆ built-up using a task procedure costing sheet.

Figure 3.25 illustrates a task procedure sheet developed by a joinery company for assembly work. It is used as a computer spreadsheet. The task is analysed and broken down into its individual elements and entered on the sheet for a one-off. The times for each task are calculated by the software and multiplied by the batch size (number off required), giving the total assembly time required.

The actual labour cost per hour charged by a company will be far in excess of the hourly rate paid to its employees. It will be the full cost of employing a person and is made up of the following:

◆ Direct costs of employing the hourly paid operatives, mainly wood machinists and joiners, including the cost of insurance and holidays, overtime rates and bonus payments, etc.
◆ Indirect costs of employing both hourly paid operatives, such as general operatives and packing/despatch operatives, etc. Salaried staff including workshop foreman, managers, the setter/marker-out and other technical staff, again including the cost of insurance and holidays, etc.

The typical cost of employing a person is two to three times the hourly rate paid and this does not include other overheads and profit.

Each firm will have its own system for recording the amount of time spent by hourly paid operatives on a particular task. Typical methods of time collection include (see Figure 3.26):

◆ Job records showing who has worked on a particular job. These are completed by the foreman.
◆ Timesheets kept by individual operatives, showing on a daily basis the type and duration of tasks undertaken.
◆ Electronic smartcards, which are being used increasingly even by smaller concerns. The card is 'swiped' into the system by operatives who enter a job code each time they undertake a different task.

In addition to determining the labour cost of a job, the information collected may also be used to:

◆ compare the actual cost with the estimated cost;
◆ compile standard times for tasks;
◆ compare individual performance against a standard time;
◆ calculate financial incentive scheme payments;
◆ compile statistical information on productivity and downtime.

Overall costs – overheads and profits are added to the actual material and labour costs to determine the total price charged to the customer for a particular job. Typical costs recovered in overheads are:

◆ salaries of administrative staff, senior support staff and directors;
◆ building maintenance and running costs;
◆ plant and machinery costs;
◆ consumable material costs.

ENTER TIMES FOR A 1 OFF ASSEMBLED, SHEET WILL ADJUST FOR BATCH QUANTITY

DESCRIPTION	
PART NUMBER	
QUANTITY	

JOINERY ASSEMBLY

ACTIVITY	QTY	DESCRIPTION	MEASURE	Mins	TOTAL Mins
GENERAL ASSEMBLY Pick up and position component part		LARGE - ABOVE 1 m	PER PIECE	1.00	
		MEDIUM - ABOVE 0.5 m	PER PIECE	0.70	
		SMALL - BELOW 0.5 m	PER PIECE	0.35	
Framed joints		FIT SINGLE MORTISE AND TENON JOINT	PER JOINT	2.25	
		HAND SCRIBE OR MITRE MOULDING AT JOINT	PER JOINT	3.00	
FIXINGS Nails/Pins/Dowels		GLUE AND POSITION WOODEN DOWEL	PER OCCASION	0.50	
		INSERT PIN OR NAIL	PER OCCASION	0.25	
		FILL PIN OR NAIL HOLE USING FILLER, INC SAND OFF	PER OCCASION	0.30	
Screws		POSITION AND SECURE SCREW	PER SCREW	0.50	
		FILL SCREW HOLE USING PELLET, INC SAND OFF	PER SCREW HOLE	1.25	
HAND & POWER TOOLS		USE CHOP SAW	PER CUT	0.75	
		USING POWER ROUTER	PER LIN M	1.25	
		USE HAND PLANE	PER LIN M	1.00	
		CUT GROOVE, APPLY GLUE, FIT BISCUIT	PER BISCUIT	1.25	
GLUE & CRAMPS		APPLY GLUE - PER BEAD	PER LIN M	0.75	
		SECURE AND REMOVE CRAMP	PER OCCASION	1.25	
Drawer		ASSEMBLE AND FIT DRAWER	PER ASSEMBLY	22.00	
Unit doors		ASSEMBLE AND FIT SWING DOOR TO UNIT	PER DOOR	12.50	
		ASSEMBLE AND FIT SLIDING DOORS TO UNIT	PER PAIR	14.75	
Building door		HANG C/W 2 No HINGES, LEVER FURN, AND LOCK/LATCH	PER DOOR	85.00	
IRONMONGERY Unit handles		FIT "D" TYPE HANDLE	EACH	2.10	
Unit catch		FIT BALESOR MAG. CATCH	EACH	2.50	
Surface bolt		FIT TOWER BOLT	EACH	2.75	
Additional hinges		FLUSH HINGE	PER HINGE	1.25	
		BUTT HINGE	PER HINGE	2.50	
		PIANO HINGE	PER LIN M	17.25	
Glass & metalwork		UNWRAP AND POSITION	PER ITEM	1.50	
SANDING & FINISHING		SAND – FACE	PER SQ. MTR	9.25	
		SAND – EDGE OR DE-ARRIS EDGE	PER LIN. MTR.	0.50	
LAMINATE & EDGING		APPLY FACE LAMINATE	PER SQ. MTR	30.00	
		APPLY LAMINATE EDGING	PER LIN. MTR.	12.50	
		APPLY TAPE EDGING (brush glue or iron-on)	PER LIN. MTR.	7.50	
		APPLY TIMBER EDGING	PER LIN. MTR.	17.50	
ESTIMATED ITEMS		DESCRIPTION	UNIT	TIME	
Estimated time for work required, but not included in sheet					
EXAMINE & LABEL		EXAMINE, AFFIX QUALITY LABEL TRANSFER TO PALLET	PER OCCASION	2.50	
OCCASIONAL ELEMENTS		Receive parts, ironmongery, check measurements, cutting list, plan method and sequence of work, consult on details, rectify faults, sort tools on bench or at workplace, turn work over or around on bench or workplace, examine assembly, machine items – grind off hardware to fit, find tools, pallets etc and clock on and off.	Percentage already included in rates shown above		

TOTAL MINS PER ITEM

TOTAL MINS FOR COMPLETE BATCH QUANTITY

TOTAL HOURS FOR COMPLETE BATCH QUANTITY

Figure 3.25 *Typical computer-based joinery task procedure - costing spreadsheet*

Marking out for Joinery

Chapter 3

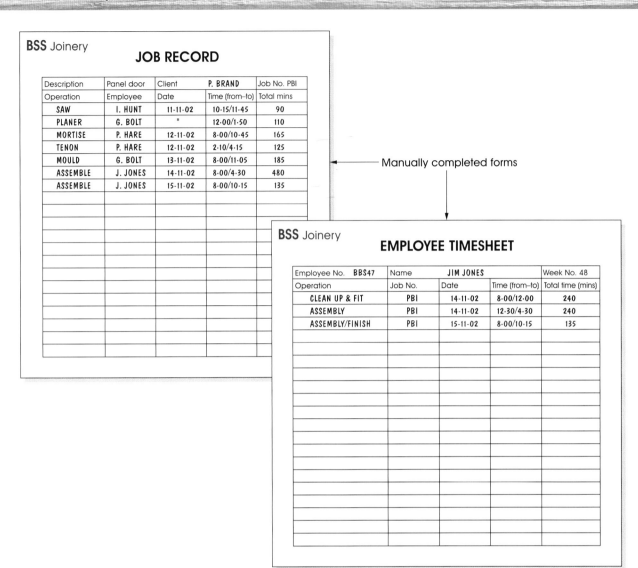

BSS Joinery

JOB RECORD

Description	Panel door	Client	**P. BRAND**	Job No. PBI
Operation	Employee	Date	Time (from–to)	Total mins
SAW	I. HUNT	11-11-02	10·15/11·45	90
PLANER	G. BOLT	"	12·00/1·50	110
MORTISE	P. HARE	12-11-02	8·00/10·45	165
TENON	P. HARE	12-11-02	2·10/4·15	125
MOULD	G. BOLT	13-11-02	8·00/11·05	185
ASSEMBLE	J. JONES	14-11-02	8·00/4·30	480
ASSEMBLE	J. JONES	15-11-02	8·00/10·15	135

Manually completed forms

BSS Joinery

EMPLOYEE TIMESHEET

Employee No. **BBS47**	Name	**JIM JONES**		Week No. 48
Operation	Job No.	Date	Time (from–to)	Total time (mins)
CLEAN UP & FIT	PBI	14-11-02	8·00/12·00	240
ASSEMBLY	PBI	14-11-02	12·30/4·30	240
ASSEMBLY/FINISH	PBI	15-11-02	8·00/10·15	135

BSS Joinery

BSS47 J JONES

Electronic 'smartcard' linked to computer base management information system

BOOKINGS BY JOB NUMBER   **PB1**

Operation	Centre	Date	Employee	Time Booked	Standard Time	Variance
010	Mill	11-11-02	Hunt	90	95	−5
020	Mill	11-11-02	Bolt	110	105	5
030	Mill	12-11-02	Hare	165	180	−15
040	Mill	12-11-02	Hare	125	135	−10
050	Mill	13-11-02	Bolt	185	200	−15
		Total for Mill		675	715	−40
060	Join	14-11-02	Jones	240		
060	Join	14-11-02	Jones	240		
060	Join	14-11-02	Jones	135	600	15
		Total for Joinery		615	600	15
		Total for Job		1290	1315	−25

Figure 3.26 *Time collection*

Details of a 762 × 1981 mm internal panel door are illustrated in Figure 3.27.

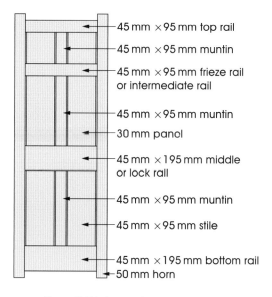

45 mm ×95 mm top rail

45 mm ×95 mm muntin

45 mm ×95 mm frieze rail or intermediate rail

45 mm ×95 mm muntin

30 mm panel

45 mm ×195 mm middle or lock rail

45 mm ×95 mm muntin

45 mm ×95 mm stile

45 mm ×195 mm bottom rail

50 mm horn

Figure 3.27 *A typical panelled door*

(a) The target time for assembling each door is 1¼ hours; determine how long it should take to assemble a batch of 15 doors.

(b) Calculate the labour cost of assembling the batch of doors, if the direct cost of employing a joiner is £21.50 per hour and the company adds on an overhead of 42% for indirect costs and profit.

(c) Copy and complete the blank joinery method statement (Figure 3.28) to provide a guide for the joiners who are going to assemble the doors.

(d) Calculate the total volume and cost of 50 × 100 mm and 50 × 200 mm sawn US redwood required to produce the rails, stiles and muntings for the entire batch of doors. Include an allowance of 10% for cutting and wastage and use a rate £225.75 per m³.

(e) Copy and complete the blank order/requisition (Figure 3.29) for the volume of softwood required using the following:

◆ Order number POD/425
◆ From: Lawcris Timber Supplies
  Lawcris Yard
  Fields Farm Road
  Nottingham NG9 4XY
◆ Deliver to: BBS Joinery
  Long Eaton
  Nottingham NG10 2DA
  Date required: 26 Aug 2007

Marking out for Joinery

Chapter 3

JOINERY METHOD STATEMENT

Works Order Number		Del. Date	

Description	

Part Number	

Client	

Unit Time hrs		Quantity	

Total Time hrs	

No.	Operations									
1										
2										
3										
4										
5										
6										
7										
8										
9										
10										

Figure 3.28 *Joinery method statement*

BBS CONSTRUCTION
ORDER/REQUISITION

Registered office

No. _____

Date _____

To _____ From _____

Address ————————— Site address —————————

_____ _____

Please supply or order for delivery to the above site the following:

Description	Quantity	Rate	Date required by

Site manager/foreman _____

Note Please advise site within 24 hours of request if order cannot be fulfilled by the date requested

Figure 3.29 *Order/requisition form*

measuring up

1. Define the term 'marking out' and state how it differs from setting out.

2. Explain the reason for using patterns when marking out joinery components.

3. Briefly describe TWO main considerations made before placing a face mark on a piece of timber.

4. The tool/piece of equipment best used when squaring over lines on a pre-moulded piece of timber is: (a) steel square; (b) combination square; (c) box square; (d) set square.

5. Produce a sketch to show the veneer arrangement for a table top that is specified as quarter matched.

6. State the reason why a batch of paired stiles may be cramped to the pattern for marking out.

7. Explain why radial sawn timber sections are more stable than tangential sawn sections.

8. Define the following terms related to stair construction: margin; rise; going.

9. Sketch a typical pattern head for an external door frame, marked up ready for machining.

10. State how the best possible grain match could be achieved for the meeting stiles of a pair of doors that are to receive a clear finish.

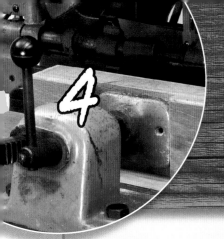

4

Manufacture of Joinery Products

This chapter is intended to provide the reader with an overview of the manufacture and assembly of routine joinery products. Its contents are assessed in the **NVQ Unit VR 16 Manufacture Routine Products.**

In this chapter you will cover the following range of topics:

- ◆ task planning;
- ◆ windows;
- ◆ doors;
- ◆ door ironmongery;
- ◆ door frames and linings;
- ◆ door sets;
- ◆ stairs;
- ◆ units and fitments.

What is required in VR 16?

To successfully complete this unit you will be required to demonstrate your skill and knowledge of the following bench joinery processes:

- ◆ interpreting information;
- ◆ adopting safe and healthy working practices;
- ◆ selecting materials, components and equipment;
- ◆ fit and assemble internal and external joinery products.

You will be required practically to:

- ◆ fit, assemble and finish components for a range of joinery products including:
  - ▶ doors
  - ▶ frames (glazed and non-glazed)
  - ▶ linings
  - ▶ units and/or fitments
  - ▶ staircases;
- ◆ use hand tools, power tools and workshop equipment;
- ◆ take workplace dimensions;
- ◆ requisition materials;
- ◆ communicate with other team members, including setter-out/marker-out, machinists and other joiners;
- ◆ undertake calculations for quantity, measurement or costs.

Task planning

Pre-task work

Before starting a job you will be involved in planning and organising the work. You may ask yourself the following questions:

◆ What is to be done?
◆ How is it to be done?
◆ When is it to be done?
◆ Where is it to be done?

In answering these questions, which is part of the planning process, you will refer to: drawings, specifications, setting-out rods, method statements and the actual machined components, etc. Any discrepancies must be resolved before proceeding with the work, as any mistakes are more costly to rectify the further they go unnoticed.

Depending on your employer's line of communication, this may be directed via your workshop foreman/manager or direct with the setter-out/marker-out.

The means of communication will again vary depending on your organisation's line of communication and may involve direct face-to-face contact, a telephone call, e-mail or memo, or use of a standard form. The spoken word is often used as a quick and informal first point of contact. However, a written confirmation should be sought as evidence and as a means of updating information for the future.

Figure 4.1 *Pre-task planning*

Resolving irregularities

On checking the machined components with the drawings and details, you notice that the data sheet for a veneered standard shows a vertical grain direction, whereas, the actual standard has been machined with a horizontal grain direction (see Figure 4.2).

Your first action should be to speak directly or via the telephone with either your foreman/manager or setter-out/marker-out, to find whether there has been a last-minute change or the standard has been incorrectly machined.

If the data sheet has been revised and the grain direction as machined is correct, a new data sheet should be issued as confirmation.

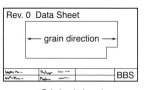

did you know?

You should resolve any irregularities at the earliest possible time to avoid unnecessary work.

Original sheet

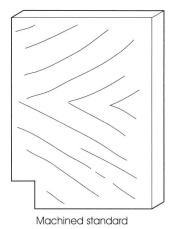
Machined standard

Figure 4.2 *Irregularities between data sheet and cut panel*

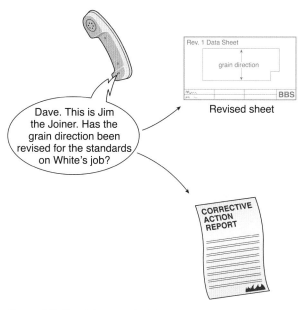

Figure 4.3 *Resolving irregularities*

Manufacture of Joinery Products

Chapter 4

If the data sheet is correct you may be required to complete a corrective action report form. This will have the effect of reordering the 'incorrectly' machined part (see Figure 4.4).

BSS Joinery

CORRECTIVE ACTION REPORT

Raised by:	JIM. JONES	Job number:	WC12	Date raised:	8-11-02
Description:	BASE UNIT			Client:	WHITES & CO.

Defect or Improvement					
Manufacturing		Design		Details	
Saw:		Drawings:		General:	
Plane:		Specification:		DATA SHEET FOR STANDARD,	
Joint:		Data sheet:		SHOWS VERTICAL GRAIN, BUT HAS	
Mould:		Method statement:		BEEN CUT HORIZONTALLY. CHECKED	
Bore:		Setting out:		WITH DESIGN, DATA SHEET IS	
Assembly:		Marking out:		CORRECT.	
Handling damage:		Improvement:			
Other:	✔	Other:			
Suggested Corrective Action: (originator to complete)				Issued to:	
RE-MACHINE 10 NEW STANDARDS TO DATA SHEET. _J.J._				MACHINE SHOP	
				Data received:	
Corrective Action Taken: (recipient to complete)				Action taken by:	
				Data completed:	

☑ Tick appropriate box

Figure 4.4
*Corrective action
report form*

Checking components

All materials and ironmongery should be inspected before use:

- Check you have the correct number of components shown on the cutting list.
- Inspect all components for damage. Any scratches on sheet material or bowing, shakes and other defect in timber, should be brought to the attention of your foreman/manager, who will decide whether they are acceptable for use or require replacement.
- Ensure all ironmongery and other fittings are as specified and working correctly. Return defective items to the store for replacement.

Work tasks

Look at the method statement if provided, or write down a list of main tasks to be done in the order that they will be undertaken.

example
- Apply hardwood edge to batch of worktops and overlay with laminate.
- Mitre edging at returns.
- Glue and loose tongue, edge to top.
- Clean edge flush with face.
- Overlay with laminate.
- Trim off laminate and profile edge
- Sand up edging ready for finishing.

The entire order of 50 carcass units is required for completion on or before 5th July to enable delivery on the 6th.

u have an hour
o assemble a
ame and door.

Figure 4.5 *Work timing*

Tools and equipment

Look at the method statement or your work tasks list. Ensure you have all the correct specialist tools and equipment ready to undertake the task. Make a list. Items you do not have may require requisition from your stores, or even hiring from an outside supplier for the duration of the job. An example tools and equipment list is shown below.

> **example**
> ◆ Chop saw;
> ◆ 900 mm sash cramps (10 off);
> ◆ 'jay' roller;
> ◆ hand-powered router and profile cutter;
> ◆ orbital sander.

Work timing

The time required to complete a task will depend on your skill level and how familiar you are with it. You may be given either a target time to do the work or a required completion date.

You will have to consider whether you can complete the task on your own within the deadlines; if not, request assistance (Figure 4.5).

Review of task

On completion of the task, you should undertake a review. Think of any problems that occurred and steps you took to make things easier. Remember these and incorporate them in future tasks. Figure 4.6 illustrates the planning, task and review procedure.

did you know?

A review of the task after completion will help the next job.

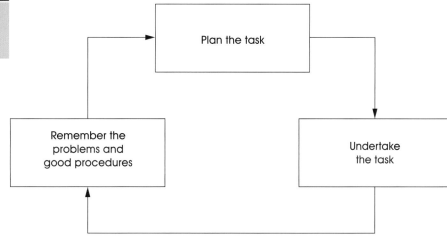

Figure 4.6 *Planning, task and review procedure*

Manufacture of Joinery Products

Chapter 4

Windows

A window is a glazed opening in a wall used to admit daylight and air and also to give the building's occupants an outside view. They are classified into different types by their method of opening, which is illustrated in Figure 4.7.

◆ Casements – which are either top or side hung on hinges.
◆ Pivot hung – which can be either horizontally or vertically hung.
◆ Sliding sashes – which can slide either horizontally or vertically.

The recommended method of indicating on a drawing the type of window and its method of opening is shown in Figure 4.8.

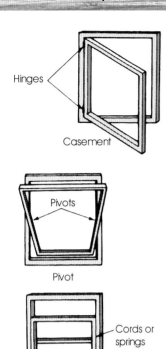

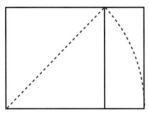

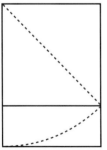

Figure 4.7 *Types of window*

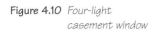

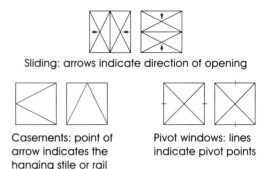

Sliding: arrows indicate direction of opening

Casements: point of arrow indicates the hanging stile or rail

Pivot windows: lines indicate pivot points

Figure 4.8 *Direction of window opening*

Figure 4.9 illustrates the principle of determining the size of rectangular window openings, with well-balanced proportions. The method used is to draw a square with sides equal to the smallest dimension and then to swing the diagonal down to give the longest side. This method is equally suitable to determine the proportions of other items of joinery where a pleasing, balanced effect is required.

Casement windows

A casement window comprises of two main parts: the frame and opening casement or casement sash.

The frame consists of head, sill and two jambs. Where the frame is subdivided, the intermediate vertical members are called mullions and the intermediate horizontal member is called a transom.

The opening casement consists of top rail, bottom rail and two stiles. Where the casement is subdivided, both the intermediate vertical and horizontal members are called glazing bars. Opening casements that are above the transom are known as fanlights. Fixed glazing is called a dead light and glazing at the bottom of a window, normally below a casement, is a sublight. Where glass is bedded in the main frame itself, it is called direct glazing.

The elevation of a four-light casement window is shown in Figure 4.10 with all the component parts named. The 'four' refers to the number of glazed openings or lights in the window.

Figure 4.9 *Setting out rectangular openings*

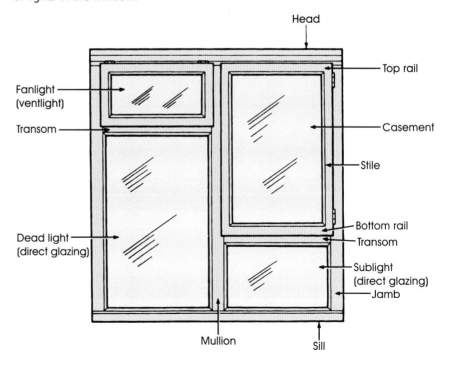

Figure 4.10 *Four-light casement window*

Casement windows can further be divided into two types, traditional and stormproof, depending on their method of construction (see Figure 4.11).

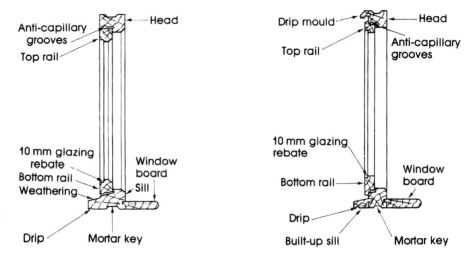

Figure 4.11 *Traditional casement and (right) stormproof casement*

Traditional casement

A vertical section through a traditional casement window is illustrated in Figure 4.12. In order to prevent the passage of water into the building, anti-capillary grooves are incorporated into the frame and the opening casements. Drip grooves are made towards the front edges of the transom and sill to stop the water running back beneath them.

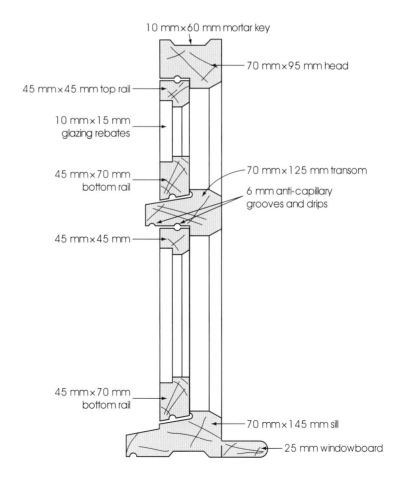

Figure 4.12 *Traditional casement window (vertical section)*

Manufacture of Joinery Products

Chapter 4

did you know?

The term 'weathered' refers to a 9° slope applied to the horizontal surfaces of external joinery to assist rainwater run off.

A mortar key groove is run on the outside face of the head, sill and jambs. The sill also has a plough groove for the window sill to tongue into. Both transom and sill incorporate a throat to check the penetration of wind-assisted rain. In addition this feature may be continued up the jambs.

Figure 4.13 is a part horizontal section through a traditional casement window. It also shows the sizes and positions of the rebates, grooves and moulding in the jambs, mullion and casement stiles.

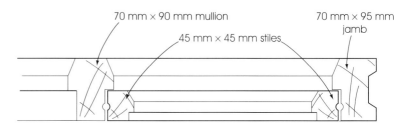

70 mm × 90 mm mullion 45 mm × 45 mm stiles 70 mm × 95 mm jamb

Figure 4.13 *Traditional casement window (part horizontal section)*

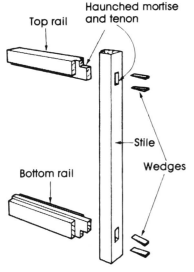

Top rail Haunched mortise and tenon Stile Bottom rail Wedges

Figure 4.14 *Haunched mortise and tenon joint secured with wedges*

All joints used in traditional casement window construction are mortise and tenons. Standard haunched mortise and tenons (Figure 4.14) are generally used for the actual casements, although a sash haunch (Figure 4.15) is preferable where smaller sections are used. As a matter of good practice, the depth of the rebates should be kept the same as the depth of the mouldings. This simplifies the jointing as the shoulders of the tenons will be level.

The jointing of head, jamb and sill of the main frame are mortise and tenons (see Figure 4.16). These joints are normally wedged, although the use of draw pins or star dowels is acceptable and even preferable where the horn is to be cut off later. In addition, by offsetting the hole in the tenon slightly towards the shoulder, the joint will be drawn up tight as the pin is driven in (see Figure 4.17).

In order to make a better weatherproof joint, the front edge of the transom is housed across the jamb (see Figure 4.18).

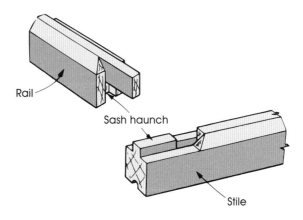

Rail Sash haunch Stile

Figure 4.15 *Joint detail (sash haunch)*

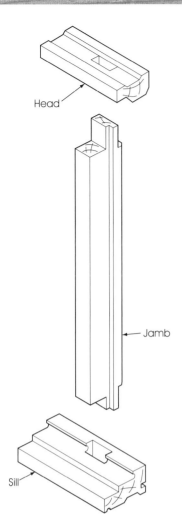

Head

Jamb

Sill

Figure 4.16 *Main frame joints*

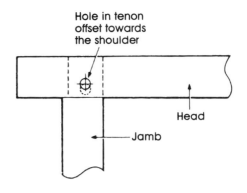

Hole in tenon
offset towards
the shoulder

Head

Jamb

Figure 4.17 *Draw pinning*

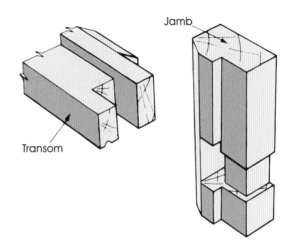

Jamb

Transom

Figure 4.18 *Transom joint details*

Manufacture of Joinery Products **Chapter 4**

Stormproof casement

Stormproof casement windows incorporate two rebates, one round the main frame, and the other round the casement. These rebates, in conjunction with the drip, anti-capillary grooves and throat, make this type far more weatherproof than traditional casements (see Figure 4.19).

The jointing of the main frame of the stormproof casement window is often the same as that of the traditional casement, except for the transom, which is not housed across the face of the jambs since it is usually of the same width. Comb joints can also be used, although they leave no horn for building in. Comb joints fixed with metal star dowels (see Figure 4.20) are normally used for jointing the actual casements, although mortise-and-tenon joints can be used.

Assembly procedure

The main frame and casement should be assembled dry to check the fit of joints, sizes, square and winding.

Squaring up of a frame is checked with a squaring rod, which consists of a length of rectangular section timber with a panel pin in its end, as shown in Figure 4.21. The end with a panel pin is placed in one corner of the frame (see Figure 4.22). The length of the diagonal should then be marked in pencil on the rod. The other diagonal should then be checked. If the pencil marks occur in the same place, the frame must be square. If the frame is not square, then sash cramps should be angled to pull the frame into square, as shown in Figure 4.23.

did you know?

Adjustment to the joints may be required if a frame is distorted.

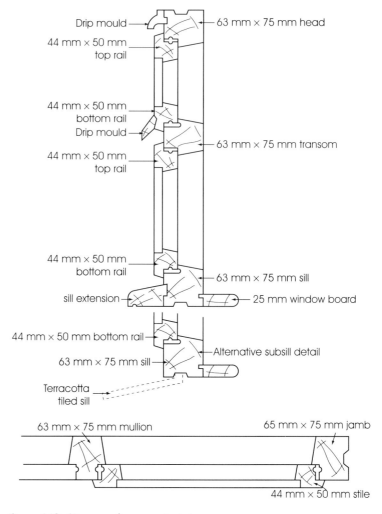

Drip mould
44 mm × 50 mm top rail
44 mm × 50 mm bottom rail
Drip mould
44 mm × 50 mm top rail
44 mm × 50 mm bottom rail
sill extension

63 mm × 75 mm head
63 mm × 75 mm transom
63 mm × 75 mm sill
25 mm window board

44 mm × 50 mm bottom rail
63 mm × 75 mm sill
Terracotta tiled sill
Alternative subsill detail

63 mm × 75 mm mullion
65 mm × 75 mm jamb
44 mm × 50 mm stile

Figure 4.19 *Stormproof casement window*

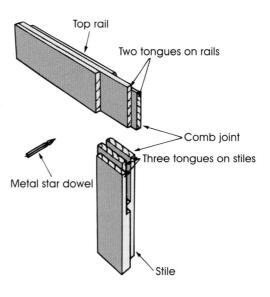

Top rail
Two tongues on rails
Comb joint
Three tongues on stiles
Metal star dowel
Stile

Figure 4.20 *Comb joint secured with a metal star dowel*

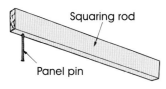

Squaring rod

Panel pin

Figure 4.21 *Squaring rod*

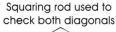

Squaring rod used to
check both diagonals

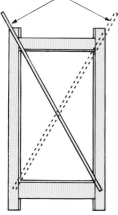

Figure 4.22 *Checking the frame
for square*

Squaring rod used to
check both diagonals

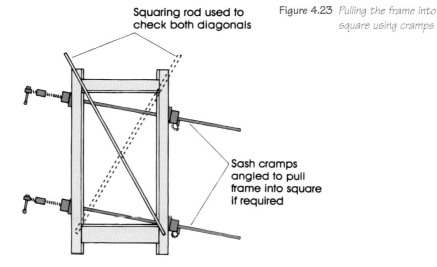

Sash cramps
angled to pull
frame into square
if required

Figure 4.23 *Pulling the frame into
square using cramps*

Winding of a frame is checked with winding strips. These are two parallel pieces of timber. With the frame laying flat on a level bench, place a winding strip at either end of the job. Close one eye and sight the tops of the two strips as shown in Figure 4.24. If they appear parallel, the frame is flat or 'out of wind'. The frame is said to be winding, in wind or distorted if the two strips do not line up. Repositioning of the cramps or adjustment to the joints may be required.

Glue up – assemble and lightly drive wedges (see Figure 4.25). A waterproof adhesive should be used for external joinery or where it is likely to be used in a damp location. Ensure the overall sizes are within the stated tolerances. Re-check for square and wind. Assuming all is correct, finally drive wedges and insert star dowels as appropriate.

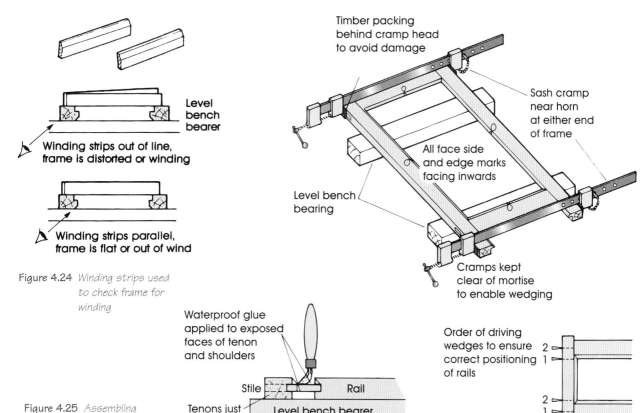

Level
bench
bearer

◢ **Winding strips out of line,
frame is distorted or winding**

◢ **Winding strips parallel,
frame is flat or out of wind**

Figure 4.24 *Winding strips used
to check frame for
winding*

Timber packing
behind cramp head
to avoid damage

Sash cramp
near horn
at either end
of frame

All face side
and edge marks
facing inwards

Level bench
bearing

Cramps kept
clear of mortise
to enable wedging

Waterproof glue
applied to exposed
faces of tenon
and shoulders

Stile   Rail

Figure 4.25 *Assembling
casement sash*

Tenons just
inserted

Level bench bearer

Order of driving
wedges to ensure
correct positioning
of rails

2
1

2
1

Manufacture of Joinery Products

Chapter 4

did you know?

You should always keep cramps clear of mortises to enable wedging up.

Hanging casement sashes

Stormproof casements fit on the face of the frame and normally require no fitting at all. The only operation necessary to hang the casement is the screwing on of the hinges (see Figure 4.26).

Traditional casements fit inside the frame and require both fitting and hanging. This is often thought of as a difficult task but by following the procedure given and illustrated in Figure 4.27, the task is greatly simplified.

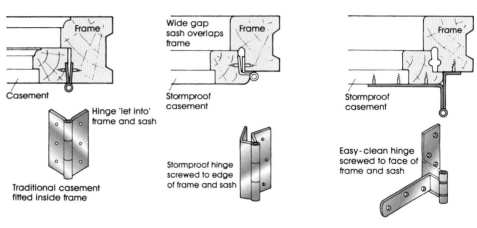

Figure 4.26 *Hanging of casement sashes*

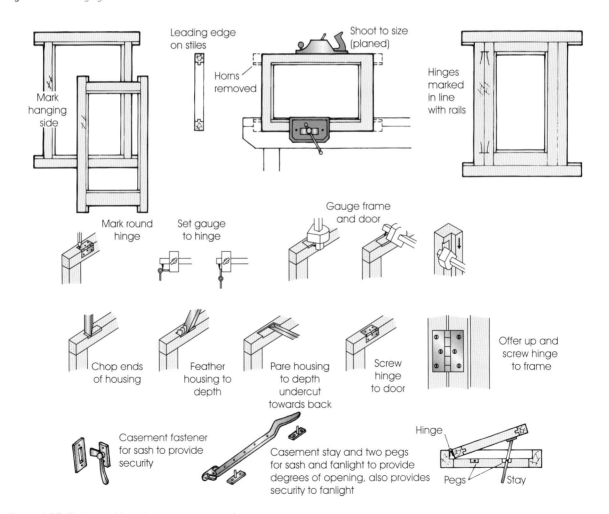

Figure 4.27 *Fitting and hanging a casement sash*

Fitting and hanging procedure:

1. Mark the hanging side on both the sash and the frame.
2. Cut off the horns.
3. 'Shoot in' (plane to fit) the hanging stile.
4. Shoot the sash to width.
5. Shoot in the top and bottom of the sash.
6. Mark out and cut in the hinges.
7. Screw one leaf of the hinges to the sash.
8. Offer up the sash to the opening and screw the other leaf to the frame.
9. Adjust fit if required and fix any other ironmongery.

When planed, the two stiles should have a 'leading edge' (slightly out of square). This allows the sash to close freely without binding. The joint on casements should be 2 mm. This is to allow a certain amount of moisture movement and to prevent the casement from jamming in the frame.

Pivot windows

The vertical and horizontal sections of a traditional pivot window is shown in Figure 4.28. Both the surrounding frame and the pivoting sash are constructed using mortises and tenons. The sash is hung on pivot pins about 25 mm above its centre line height to give it a self-closing tendency. The pivot pin is usually fixed to the frame and the socket to the sash. The planted stops that form the rebates serve to weatherproof the window. Those above the pivots are nailed or screwed to the frame on the outside and the sash on the inside, whereas those below are fixed to the frame on the inside and the sash on the outside. The actual positions of intersections of the beads needs to be determined precisely, especially where the sash is required to be removable without taking off any beads. This is shown in the vertical section. The sash stile and its planted top bead must be grooved, as shown, to allow removal of the sash. The head and top rail are splayed to give sufficient opening clearance. This is provided at the sill by its weathering.

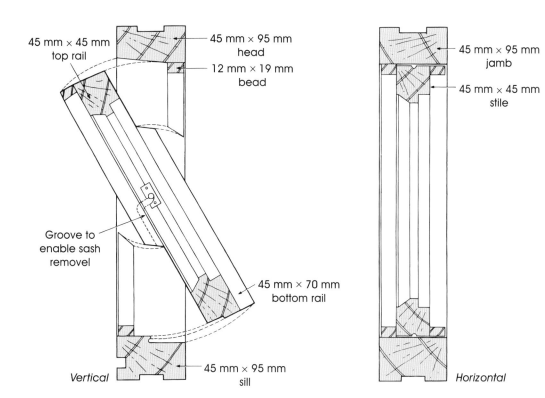

Vertical

45 mm × 45 mm top rail

45 mm × 95 mm head

12 mm × 19 mm bead

Groove to enable sash removel

45 mm × 70 mm bottom rail

45 mm × 95 mm sill

Horizontal

45 mm × 95 mm jamb

45 mm × 45 mm stile

Figure 4.28 *Traditional pivot window sections*

Manufacture of Joinery Products

Chapter 4

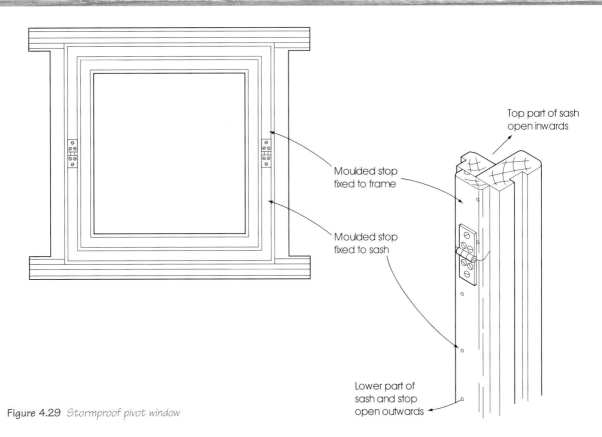

Top part of sash open inwards

Moulded stop fixed to frame

Moulded stop fixed to sash

Lower part of sash and stop open outwards

Figure 4.29 *Stormproof pivot window*

Stormproof pivot window – details of a stormproof centre-hung pivot window are shown in Figure 4.29. This is an improvement on the type described above. The joints used in the frame are mortise and tenons. Comb joints are used for the sash. Face-fixing friction pivots or back flap hinges are used for hanging the sash.

The moulded stop, which is mitred around the frame and cut on the pivot line, is glued and pinned to the top half of the frame and the bottom half of the sash.

Sash windows

Vertical sliding sashes

These consist of two sashes that slide up and down in a main frame. They are also known as double-hung sliding-sash windows. There are two different forms of construction for these types of window: those with boxed frames and those with solid frames.

Boxed frame sash windows – this type of window is the traditional pattern of sliding sashes and for many years has been superseded by casements and solid frame sash windows. This was mainly due to the high manufacturing and assembly costs of the large number of component parts. An understanding of their construction and operation is essential as they will be encountered frequently in renovation and maintenance work.

The double-hung boxed window consists of two sliding sashes suspended on cords that run over pulleys and are attached to counterbalanced weights inside the boxed frame.

Figure 4.30 shows an elevation, horizontal and vertical section of a boxed-frame sliding-sash window. It shows the make-up of this type of window and names the component parts.

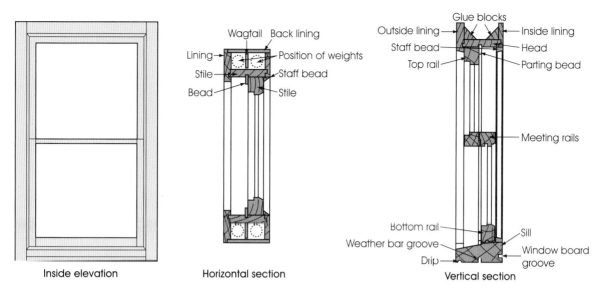

Glue blocks
Outside lining — Inside lining
Staff bead — Head
Top rail — Parting bead

Wagtail   Back lining
Lining — Position of weights
Stile — Staff bead
Bead — Stile

Meeting rails

Bottom rail — Sill
Weather bar groove — Window board groove
Drip

Inside elevation   Horizontal section   Vertical section

Figure 4.30 *Boxed frame sliding sash window details*

Solid frame sash windows – the elevation, horizontal and vertical section of a solid frame sliding sash window are illustrated in Figure 4.31. Both the frame and sashes can be jointed using mortise-and-tenon joints, or alternatively comb joints held with metal star dowels. For lightweight domestic sashes, the spring balances are accompanied in grooves run in the back of the sash stiles. The spring balances for heavyweight industrial sashes are accommodated in grooves that are run in the actual jamb of the frame.

Glazing to windows

Windows are single or double glazed using clear or patterned (obscure) glass. Glazing to windows below 800 mm from the floor level should be a safety glass that will not produce pointed shards with razor shape edges if broken. It is also recommended that environmental control glass be used. In temperate climates with cool winters such as in the UK where thermal insulation is most important, low emissivity (Low E) glass is used. This has a coating that allows heat from the sun to enter the building but reduces the amount of heat loss the other way, from inside the building. It is used mainly as the inner pane of double-glazed windows with the coated side facing into the gap or air space. In warmer climates a solar control glass may be used to limit the amount of heat gain from the sun into the building.

◆ *Single glazing* has been traditionally used for windows, 4 mm or 6 mm thickness glass being the norm, which is held in position with either putty or glazing beads (see Figure 4.31).
◆ *Double glazing* is now preferred as it offers higher levels of both thermal and sound insulation. In addition, as the temperature of the inner pane is warmer, the risk of condensation on the room side is reduced. This can be achieved using either sealed double-glazing units, or secondary glazing. *Sealed glazing units* are used to double-glaze windows for thermal insulation purposes. They consist of two panels of glass with a gap of around 25 mm between them. The panes are held apart by a spacer that runs around the perimeter and is sealed to provide an airtight joint. The units are assembled in a clean dry atmosphere or an inert gas is used to fill the gap to avoid any possibility of condensation forming between the panes (see Figure 4.32). In addition the greater mass of sealed units compared to single-glazing, will reduce to some extent the passage of sound.

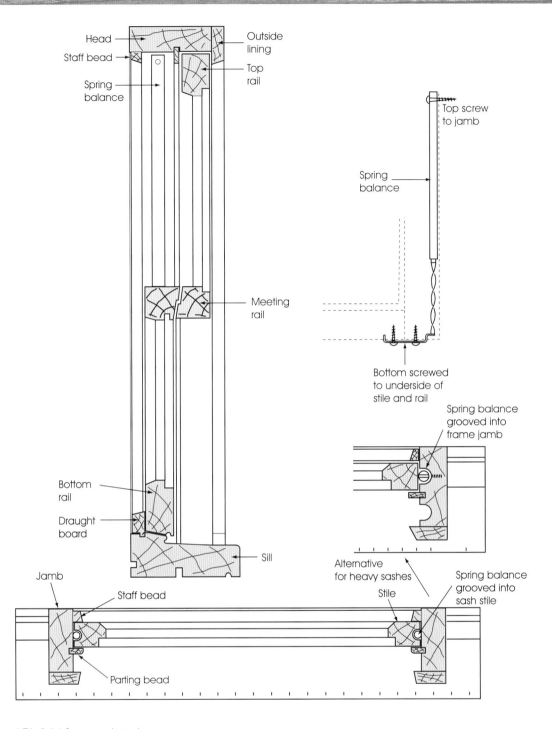

Figure 4.31 *Solid frame sash window*

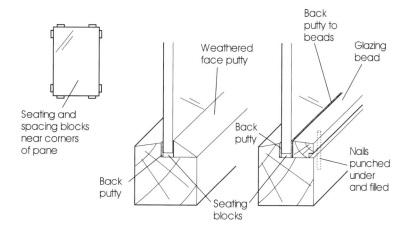

Seating and spacing blocks near corners of pane

Back putty

Weathered face putty

Back putty

Seating blocks

Back putty to beads

Glazing bead

Nails punched under and filled

Figure 4.32 *Single glazing*

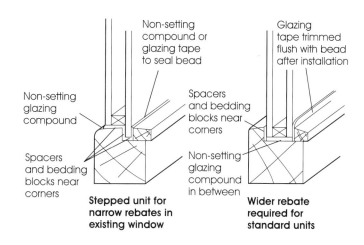

Non-setting glazing compound

Spacers and bedding blocks near corners

Non-setting compound or glazing tape to seal bead

Spacers and bedding blocks near corners

Non-setting glazing compound in between

Stepped unit for narrow rebates in existing window

Glazing tape trimmed flush with bead after installation

Wider rebate required for standard units

Figure 4.33 *Double glazing*

measuring up

1. Name a suitable piece of ironmongery for the fastening of:
   (a) a top-hung casement;
   (b) a side-hung casement sash.

2. Outline a typical procedure to follow for resolving irregularities in work documentation.

3. Name the intermediate vertical member used to divide a casement window frame.

4. State the reason for draw-pinning mortise-and-tenon joints.

5. Name the type of tenon shown in Figure 4.34.

6. State the reason why the stiles of a traditional casement window sash are planed with a 'leading edge'.

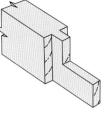
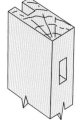

Figure 4.34 *Tenon*

7. Complete a work task list as part of your pre-task planning to show the sequence of main operations required to assemble and complete a casement window frame and sash.

8. Complete an equipment list for the task in Question 7.

9. Copy this outline of a casement window and mark the hinge positions.

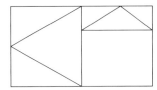

10. Sketch or describe the following terms: (a) weathering; (b) throating; (c) rebate; (d) groove.

Doors

A door is a moveable barrier used to cover an opening in a structure. Its main function is to allow access into a building and passage between the interior spaces. Other functional requirements may include weather protection, fire resistance, sound and thermal insulation, security, privacy, ease of operation and durability. Doors may be classified by their method of construction: matchboarded, panelled, glazed, flush, fire resistant, etc. (see Figure 4.35), and also by their method of operation: swinging, sliding and folding.

Methods of construction

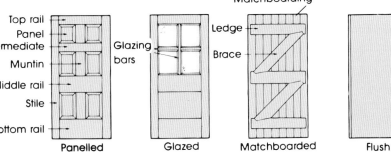
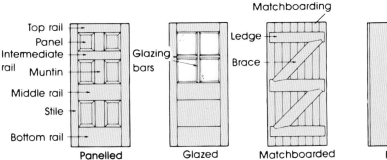

Figure 4.35 *Doors*

did you know?

The main function of doors is to provide access into and from a building and between its interior spaces. Sometimes access from a building may be referred to as 'egress' meaning 'the way out'

Panelled doors

These have a frame made from solid timber rails and stiles, which are jointed using either dowels or mortise and tenon joints. The frame is either grooved or rebated to receive two or more thin plywood or timber panels. Interior doors are thinner than exterior doors.

Glazed doors

These are used where more light is required. They are made similar to panelled doors except glass replaces one or more of the plywood or timber panels. Glazing bead is used to secure the glass into its glazing rebates. Glazing bars may be used to divide large glazed areas.

Matchboarded doors

These are used mainly externally for gates, sheds and industrial buildings. They are simply constructed from matchboarding, ledges and braces clench-nailed together. The bottom end of the braces must always point towards the hanging edge of the door to provide the required support. Framed matchboarded doors constructed with the addition of stiles and rails are used where extra strength is required.

Manufacture of Joinery Products

Chapter 4

Internal doors

Framed

Patt SA   Colonial pine   Patt 2XGG

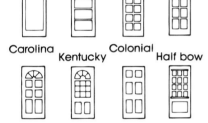

Flush

White-faced hardboard   Plywood (painted)   Sapele (polished)

Sizes available
610 mm × 1981 mm × 35 mm
686 mm × 1981 mm × 35 mm
762 mm × 1981 mm × 35 mm
865 mm × 1981 mm × 35 mm

External doors

Patt 10   Patt 50   Patt SC   Patt 8

Carolina   Kentucky   Colonial   Half bow

Sizes available
762 mm × 1981 mm × 44 mm
835 mm × 1981 mm × 44 mm
813 mm × 2032 mm × 44 mm

Figure 4.36 *Extract from a manufacturer's door list showing range of stock-size doors*

did you know?

Fire doors are commonly known as half-hour doors or one-hour doors according to the length of protection provided. These are termed in contract documents as FD30 and FD60 respectively. An 'S' suffix means it can also resist the passage of smoke, e.g. FD30S or FD60S.

Flush doors

These are made with outer faces of plywood or hardboard. Internal doors are normally lightweight, having a hollow core, solid timber edges and blocks which are used to reinforce hinge and lock positions. New flush doors will have one edge marked 'LOCK' and the other 'HINGE'; these must be followed. External and fire-resistant flush doors are much heavier, as normally they have a solid core of either timber strips or chipboard. A variation on flush doors is to use the same lightweight hollow core but have the faces covered in moulded or embossed facings to give the appearance of a traditional panel door. Internal doors use hardboard facings while plastic facings are mainly for external use.

Fire resisting doors

The main function of this type of door is to act as a barrier to a possible fire by providing the same degree of protection as the element in which it is located. They should prevent the passage of smoke, hot gases and flames for a specified period of time. This period of time will vary depending on the relevant statutory regulations and the location of the door. Fire doors are not normally purpose made, as they must have approved fire resistance certification. It is advantageous to use proven proprietary products. Oversize fire-door 'blanks' are available for cutting down to size, if required to suit specific situations.

Door sizes

All mass-produced doors may be purchased from a supplier in a range of standard sizes as shown in Figure 4.36. Special sizes or purpose made designs are normally available to order from suppliers with joinery shop contacts.

Manufacture of doors

Matchboarded doors This group of doors involves the simplest form of construction. They are suitable for both internal and external use, although they are mainly used externally for gates, sheds and industrial buildings.

Ledged and braced door The basic door shown in Figure 4.37 consists of matchboarding which is held together by ledges. This type is little used because it has a tendency to sag and distort on the side opposite the hinges.

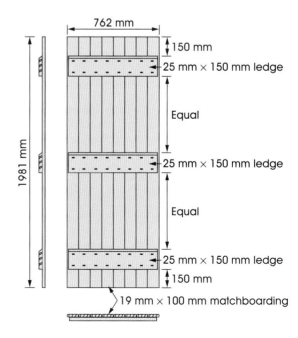

762 mm
150 mm
25 mm × 150 mm ledge
Equal
25 mm × 150 mm ledge
Equal
25 mm × 150 mm ledge
150 mm
1981 mm
19 mm × 100 mm matchboarding

Figure 4.37
Ledged and matchboarded door

In order to overcome this braces are usually incorporated in the construction (see Figure 4.38). The use of braces greatly increases the rigidity of the door. The bottom ends of the braces should always point towards the hinged edge of the door in order to provide the required support. Where these doors are used externally, the top edge of the ledges should be weathered to stop the accumulation of rainwater and moisture.

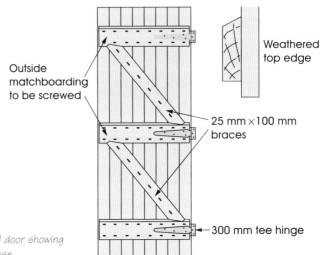

Figure 4.38 *Ledged, braced and matchboarded door showing weathering if door is for external use*

50 mm lost-head nails punched in and clenched over

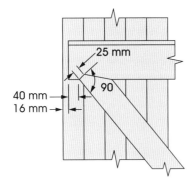

Figure 4.39 *Clenching over*

Figure 4.40 *Joint details between ledges and braces*

Three ledges are used to hold the matchboarding together. The outside pieces should be fixed with screws, while the remaining lengths of matchboarding are nailed to the ledges. Lost-head nails 6 mm longer than the thickness of the door are used for this purpose. The nails should be punched in and clenched over. Clenching over simply means bending the protruding part of the nails over and punching the ends below the surface as shown in Figure 4.39. The two braces, when used, are also fixed with lost-head nails, which are clenched over. The joint detail between the ledges and braces is shown in Figure 4.40.

Framed, ledged, braced and matchboarded door This type of door is an improvement on the ledged, braced and matchboarded door, as it includes stiles, which are jointed to the top, bottom and middle rails with mortise and tenons.

The use of the framework increases the door's strength, and resists any tendency the door might have to distort. Braces are optional when the door is framed, but their use further increases the door's strength.

Figure 4.41 shows that the stiles and top rail are the same thickness, while the middle and bottom rails are thinner. This is so that the matchboarding can be tongued into the top rail, over the face of the middle and bottom rails, and run to the bottom of the door. As the middle and bottom rails are thinner than the stiles, bare-faced tenons (tenons with only one shoulder) must be used (see Figure 4.42). These joints are normally wedged, although for extra strength draw pins can be used.

Assembly procedure for framed matchboarded doors

This is carried out using a similar procedure to that followed when assembling the casement window. Figure 4.43 shows how the stiles and rails are assembled, glued and wedged before the matchboarding is fixed.

The boards should be arranged so that the two outside ones are of equal width. They may either be tongued into the top rail and stiles or simply fit into a housing (see Figure 4.44).

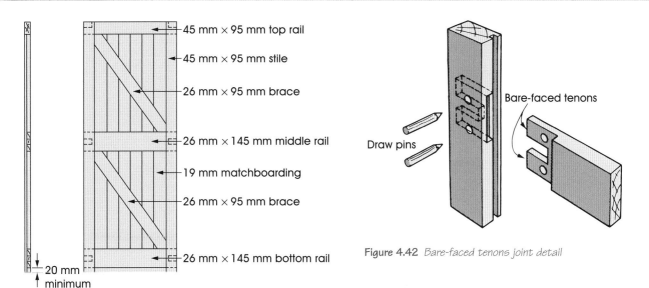

45 mm × 95 mm top rail

45 mm × 95 mm stile

26 mm × 95 mm brace

26 mm × 145 mm middle rail

19 mm matchboarding

26 mm × 95 mm brace

26 mm × 145 mm bottom rail

20 mm minimum

Figure 4.41 *Framed, ledged, braced and matchboarded door*

Bare-faced tenons

Draw pins

Figure 4.42 *Bare-faced tenons joint detail*

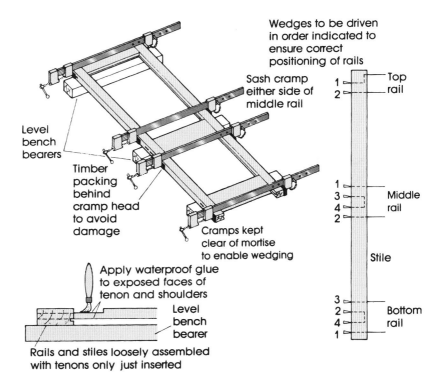

Wedges to be driven in order indicated to ensure correct positioning of rails

Sash cramp either side of middle rail

Level bench bearers

Timber packing behind cramp head to avoid damage

Cramps kept clear of mortise to enable wedging

Apply waterproof glue to exposed faces of tenon and shoulders

Level bench bearer

Rails and stiles loosely assembled with tenons only just inserted

Top rail

Middle rail

Stile

Bottom rail

Figure 4.43 *Assembling framed matchboarded door*

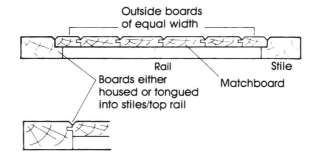

Outside boards of equal width

Rail

Stile

Matchboard

Boards either housed or tongued into stiles/top rail

Figure 4.44 *Matchboarding details*

Manufacture of Joinery Products

Chapter 4

Before assembly, the tongues and grooves, the backs of rails and braces and all other concealed surfaces must be treated with a suitable priming paint or preservative.

Arrange the boards on the assembled frame. Locate tongues and grooves so that the boards form an arc between the jambs. Place a short piece of timber across the door at either end. With assistance, apply pressure at both ends of the door to fold the boards flat (see Figure 4.45).

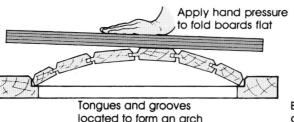 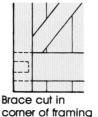 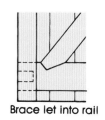

Apply hand pressure to fold boards flat

Figure 4.45
Folding matchboards and fitting braces

Tongues and grooves located to form an arch

Brace cut in corner of framing

Brace let into rail

Tap up the boards from the bottom to locate them correctly into the top rail and then clench nail or staple them (using a pneumatic nail gun) to all framing members.

Mark, cut and fix the braces. These may be either cut into the corners of the framework, or let into the rails. The cut in the corner method is simpler; however, it has a tendency to push open the joints between the stiles and the rails.

Panelled and glazed doors

The design and construction of panelled doors are very similar to glazed doors. They consist of a frame that has either a plough groove or rebate run around it to receive the panels or glazing. The framing members for these doors vary with the number and arrangements of the panels. They will consist of horizontal members and vertical members.

Rails, stiles and muntins

All horizontal members are called rails. They are also named according to their position in the door, such as top rail, middle rail, bottom rail, intermediate rail. The middle rail is also known as the lock rail and the upper intermediate rail is sometimes called a frieze rail.

The two outside vertical members are called stiles, while all intermediate vertical members are known as muntins.

Figure 4.46 shows a typical panelled door, with all its component parts named.

When using paint or other chemicals always follow the manufacturers' safety instructions concerning their use and the appropriate PPE to be worn.

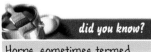
Horns, sometimes termed joggles, are the projecting ends of framed joinery.

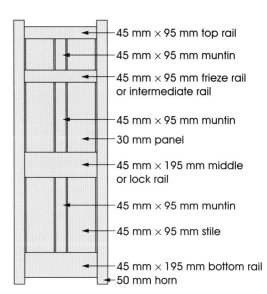

Figure 4.46
A typical panelled door

45 mm × 95 mm top rail
45 mm × 95 mm muntin
45 mm × 95 mm frieze rail or intermediate rail
45 mm × 95 mm muntin
30 mm panel
45 mm × 195 mm middle or lock rail
45 mm × 95 mm muntin
45 mm × 95 mm stile
45 mm × 195 mm bottom rail
50 mm horn

The middle and bottom rails are of a deeper section as they serve to hold the door square and thus prevent sagging. Muntins are introduced in order to reduce the panel width, therefore reducing the unsightly effect of moisture movement and the likelihood of panel damage.

It is normal to leave at least a 50 mm horn on each end of the stiles. This serves two purposes:

◆ it enables the joints to be securely wedged without fear of splitting out;
◆ the horns protect the top and bottom edges of the door before it is hung.

Panels

Figure 4.47 shows a ply panel, which is held in a plough groove that is run around the inside edge of the framing. Two ovolo mouldings are also worked around the inside edges of the framing for decorative purposes. They are known as stuck mouldings. The plough groove should be at least 2 mm deeper than the panel. This is to allow for any moisture movement (shrinkage and expansion).

Figure 4.48 again shows a solid or plywood panel, which is held in a plough groove that is run around the inside edge of the framing. Here a planted or bed mould has been applied around the panel for decoration. This method avoids the need to scribe or mitre the shoulders of the rails, which applies with stuck mouldings.

Planted moulds must not be allowed to restrict panel movement. Therefore they should be pinned to the framing and not the panel.

Figure 4.49 shows a timber panel, which is tongued into a plough groove in the framing. This type of panel is known as a bead butt panel because on its vertical edges a bead moulding is worked, while the horizontal edges remain square and butt up to the rails.

A thin plywood or glazed panel which is located in the rebate is shown in Figure 4.50. It is held in position by planted beads, which are pinned into the framing. Where this type of door is used externally water tends to get behind them. This makes both the beads and framing susceptible to decay.

For a neat finish, planted beads or moulds should not finish flush with the framing.

Figure 4.51 shows a planted mould that is rebated over the framing in order to create an enhanced feature. This type is known as a bolection mould. In general, bolection moulds are fitted on the face, and planted bed moulds on the reverse, although in the case of top-quality work bolection moulds could be used on both faces.

The bolection mould is fixed through the panel with screws. The holes for the screws should be slotted across the grain to permit panel movement without risk of splitting. The planted bed mould used on the other side to cover the screws should be skew nailed to the framing.

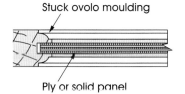

Stuck ovolo moulding

Ply or solid panel

Figure 4.47 *Panel detail (stuck moulding)*

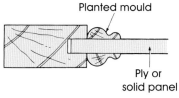

Planted mould

Ply or solid panel

Figure 4.48 *Panel detail (planted moulding)*

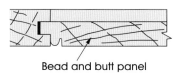

Bead and butt panel

Figure 4.49 *Panel detail (bead butt)*

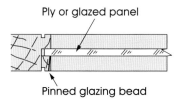

Ply or glazed panel

Pinned glazing bead

Figure 4.50 *Panel detail (planted bead)*

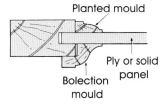

Planted mould

Ply or solid panel

Bolection mould

Figure 4.51 *Panel detail (bolection mould)*

Manufacture of Joinery Products **Chapter 4**

In good quality joinery, refurbishment or restoration work, the panels themselves may be decorated by working various mouldings on one or both of their faces. The portion around the edge of a panel is called the margin and the centre portion is known as the field. The small flat section around the edge of the panel is to enable its correct location in the framing.

Figure 4.52 illustrates the section and part elevation of the main types of decorated panels.

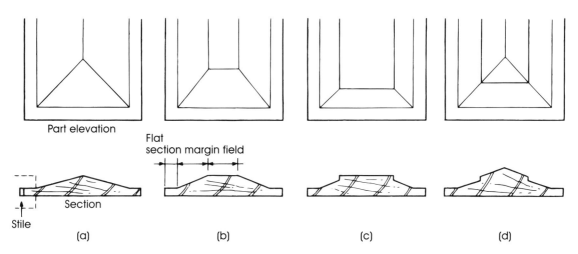

Figure 4.52 *Decorated panels: (a) raised; (b) raised and fielded; (c) raised, sunk and fielded; (d) raised, sunk and raised fielded*

(a) Shows a raised or bevel raised panel.
(b) Shows a raised and fielded panel, also known as bevel raised and fielded, where the margin has been bevelled to raise the field.
(c) Shows a raised, sunk and fielded panel, also known as bevelled, raised sunk and fielded. In this case the margin has been sunk below the field to emphasize it.
(d) Shows a raised, sunk and raised fielded panel, also known as bevelled raised, sunk and bevelled raised fielded panel, where the field itself has been bevelled as a further enhanced detail.

Where bolection moulds or planted moulds are used to finish decorated panels, the small flat section around the panel edge must be extended to provide a flat surface that will accommodate the mouldings.

Joints

Traditionally the mortise-and-tenon joint was used exclusively in the jointing of panelled and glazed doors, but today the majority of doors are mass produced and in order to reduce costs the dowelled joint is used extensively.

The use of the dowelled joint reduces the cost of the door in three ways:

◆ the length of each rail is reduced by at least 200 mm;
◆ the jointing time is reduced as holes only have to be drilled to accommodate the dowel;
◆ the assembly time is reduced as no wedging, etc., has to be carried out.

Figure 4.53 shows a six-panel door which has been jointed using dowels. These dowels should be 16 mm × 150 mm and spaced approximately 50 mm centre to centre. The following is the minimum recommended number of dowels to be used for each joint:

◆ top rail to stile: two dowels;
◆ middle rail to stile: three dowels;
◆ bottom rail to stile: three dowels;

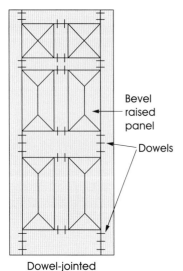

Bevel raised panel

Dowels

Dowel-jointed panel door

Figure 4.53 *Dowel-jointed panel door*

◆ intermediate rail to stile: one dowel;
◆ muntin to rail: two dowels.

Figure 4.54 shows an exploded view of a dowelled joint between a top rail and stile. In addition to the dowel, a haunch is incorporated into the joint. This ensures that the two members finish flush. Its use also overcomes any tendency for the rail to twist.

Dowels should be cut to length, chamfered off at either end to aid location and finally a small groove is formed along their length, to allow any excess glue and trapped air escape when the joint is cramped up. Alternatively 'ready-made' dowels may be used. These are available in a range of sizes; they have chamfered ends and multi-grooved sides. See Figure 4.55.

Although the dowel joint is extensively used for mass-produced doors, the mortise and tenon joint is still used widely for purpose-made and high quality door construction.

Figure 4.56 shows an exploded view of the framework for a typical six-panel door. Haunched mortise and tenons are used for the joints between the rails and stiles.

For joints between the muntins and rails, stub mortise and tenons are used. As these joints do not go right through the rails, they cannot be wedged in the normal way. Instead, fox wedges are used (see Figure 4.57). These are small wedges that are inserted into the saw cuts in the tenon. When the joint is cramped up, the wedge expands the tenon and causes it to grip securely in the mortise.

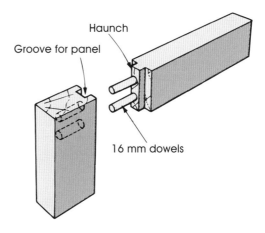

Figure 4.54 *Exploded view of a dowelled joint*

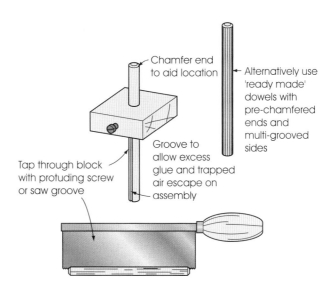

Figure 4.55 *Preparing dowels*

did you know?

Detailed procedures for cutting and wedging a range of joints is covered in a separate book titled *Wood Occupations*, also by Peter Brett.

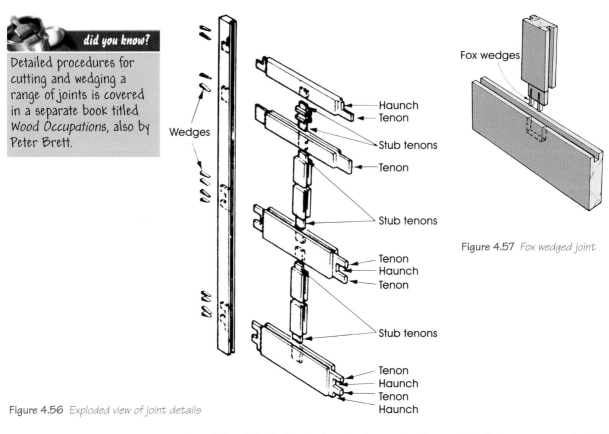

Figure 4.56 *Exploded view of joint details*

Figure 4.57 *Fox wedged joint*

A traditional half-glazed door is shown in Figure 4.58. It is constructed with diminishing stiles, in order to provide the maximum area of glass and therefore admit into the building the maximum amount of daylight. This type of door is also known as gun stock stile door because its stiles are said to resemble the stock of a gun. The middle rail has splayed shoulders to overcome the change in width of the stiles, above and below the middle rail. An exploded view of this joint is shown in Figure 4.59.

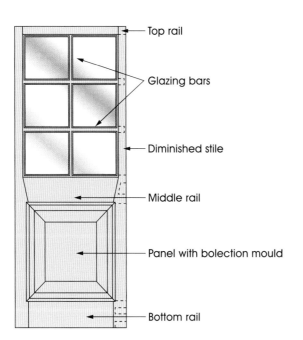

Figure 4.58 *Half-glazed door with diminishing stiles*

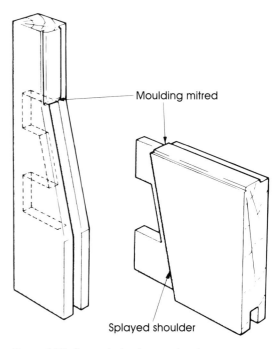

Figure 4.59 *Diminished stile joint details*

Panels in framed joinery should not be glued into the framing in order to permit differential movement between the two. If glued, the panel or framing member is liable to split.

The top half of the door can either be fully glazed or subdivided with glazing bars. When glazing bars are used they are normally stub tenoned into the stiles and rails. The joints between the glazing bars themselves could either be stub tenoned or halved and scribed (see Figure 4.60). The bottom half of the door normally consists of a bevel raised sunk and fielded panel with planted bolection mouldings.

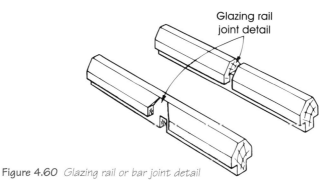

Figure 4.60 *Glazing rail or bar joint detail*

Assembly procedure for panelled and glazed doors

The following assembly procedure can be carried out for all types of framed door:

1. Dry assemble to check fit of joints, overall sizes, square and winding.
2. Clean up inside edges of all framing components and both faces of panels.
3. Glue, assemble, cramp up and wedge. Recheck for square and winding.
4. Clean up remainder of item and prepare for finishing.

The assembly of a six-panel door is illustrated in Figure 4.61. The rails and muntins should be glued and assembled first. Panels can then be inserted dry, taking care to ensure that no glue has squeezed into the panel grooves. Next, the stiles are positioned, glued, cramped and wedged, followed by final cleaning up.

Flush doors

Joinery works are rarely involved with the manufacture of flush doors, except where special features, not available in standard mass-produced doors, are required.

Figure 4.62 shows a skeleton core door, which is suitable in one-off or limited production. It consists of 28 mm × 70 mm stiles, top, bottom and middle rails; 20 mm × 28 mm intermediate rails are used to complete the framework.

Very simple joints can be used in this type of construction, as its main strength is obtained by firmly gluing the facings both to the framework and to the core. The rails are usually either tongued into a groove in the stiles or butt jointed and fixed with staples or corrugated fasteners. Ventilation holes or grooves must be incorporated between each compartment. This is to prevent air becoming trapped in the compartment when the door is assembled. If this is not done the facings will have a tendency to bulge.

Lippings

Lippings are narrow strips of timber that are fixed along the edges of better quality flush doors. Their purpose is to mask the edges of the facings and provide a neat finish to the door. External doors should have lippings fixed to all four edges for increased weather protection.

Plain lipping is acceptable for internal doors, but for better quality internal doors and external doors tongued lipping is preferred (see Figure 4.63). Lipping should be glued in position and not fixed with panel pins.

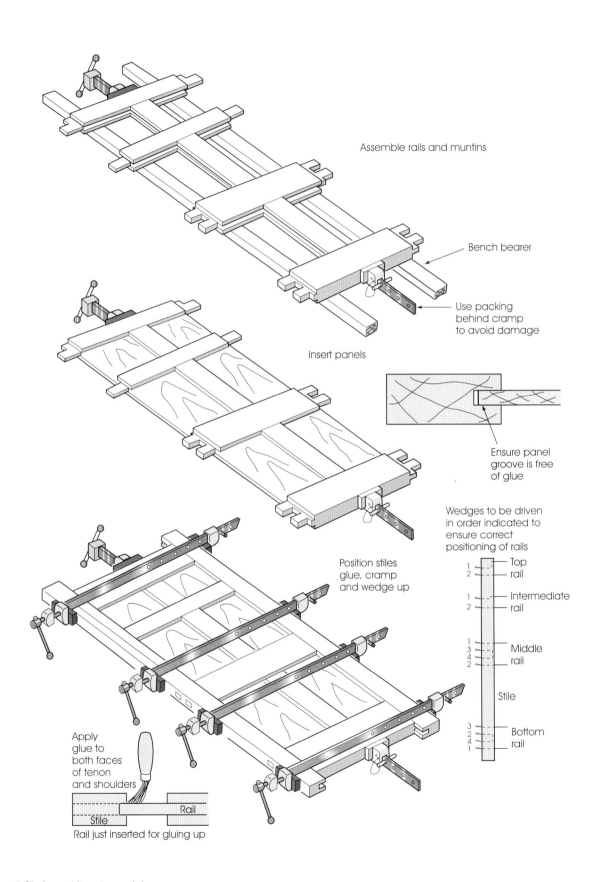

Assemble rails and muntins

Bench bearer

Use packing
behind cramp
to avoid damage

Insert panels

Ensure panel
groove is free
of glue

Wedges to be driven
in order indicated to
ensure correct
positioning of rails

Position stiles
glue, cramp
and wedge up

1
2 — Top rail

1
2 — Intermediate rail

1
3
4
2 — Middle rail

Stile

3
2
4
1 — Bottom rail

Apply
glue to
both faces
of tenon
and shoulders

Rail

Stile

Rail just inserted for gluing up

Figure 4.61 *Assembling six-panel door*

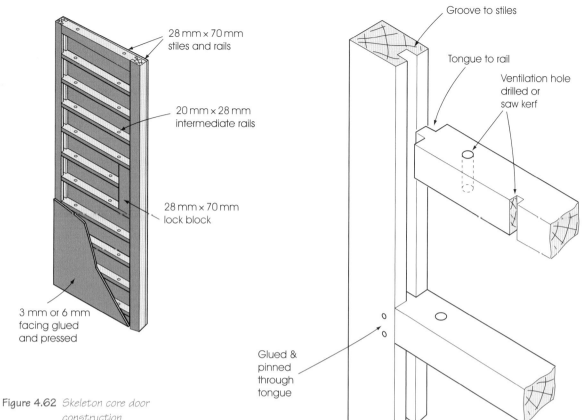

28 mm × 70 mm
stiles and rails

20 mm × 28 mm
intermediate rails

28 mm × 70 mm
lock block

3 mm or 6 mm
facing glued
and pressed

Groove to stiles

Tongue to rail

Ventilation hole
drilled or
saw kerf

Glued &
pinned
through
tongue

Figure 4.62 *Skeleton core door construction*

Figure 4.63 *Plain and tongued door lippings*

Vision panels

Vision panels are often required in purpose-made flush doors. Additional framing is required around the opening and should be as shown in Figure 4.64. Additional blocking out pieces can be used where other shaped vision panels are required (see Figure 4.65). This framing and blocking is normally done during the construction of the door, although it is possible to form the opening at a later stage.

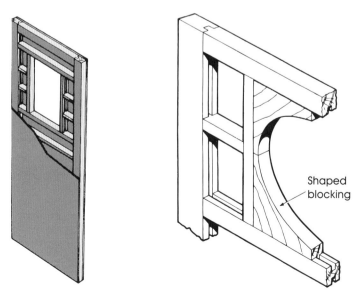

Shaped
blocking

Figure 4.64 *Flush door with vision panel*   **Figure 4.65** *Blocking for circular vision panel*

Glazings beads

Are used to hold the glass in place. Figure 4.66 shows glazing beads, suitable for an internal door. Figure 4.67 shows rebated glazing beads, which are more suitable for external doors as they provide a more weather-resistant finish. Figure 4.68 shows a better method for fixing external glazing, as it provides far greater security than the previous method.

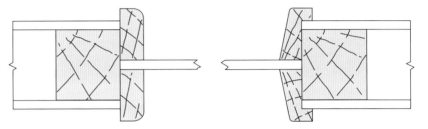

Figure 4.66 *Internal glazing beads*   Figure 4.67 *Internal or external weathered and rebated glading beads*

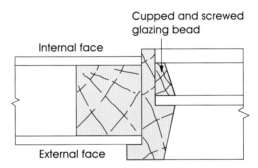

Figure 4.68 *Alternative external flush door glazing detail*

Glazing beads are normally simply pinned in place. However, for better quality work they can be fixed using countersunk brass screws and recessed cups. This enables the glazing beads to be easily removed and replaced in the event of the glass needing replacement.

Door glazing

Safety glass should be used to glaze the critical areas of doors and other vulnerable low areas, particularly where children are present The Building Regulations state that glass in these areas should break safely (it should not produce pointed shards with razor sharp edges); be robust (adequately thick to prevent the likelihood of breaking); or be permanently protected (by screens, railings or guardrails).

The critical areas and Building Regulations requirements are illustrated in Figure 4.69. Toughened and laminated glass can meet the requirements. Where annealed glass is used it must be at least 6 mm thick and in panes not larger than 0.5 m^2 with a maximum width of 250 mm. Screens, guardrails or railings on both sides, which are at least 800 mm high, should be used to permanently protect fixed annealed glass.

Methods of door operation

The main methods of door operation are swinging or side hung, sliding and folding, which are illustrated in Figure 4.70.

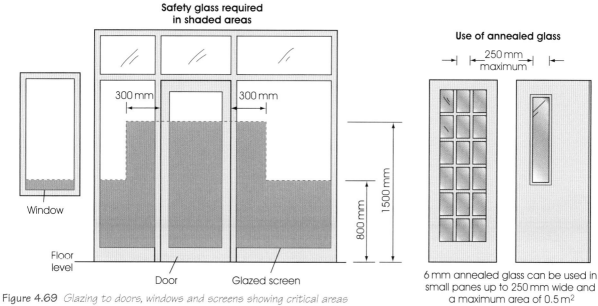

Figure 4.69 *Glazing to doors, windows and screens showing critical areas*

Use of annealed glass

6 mm annealed glass can be used in small panes up to 250 mm wide and a maximum area of 0.5 m²

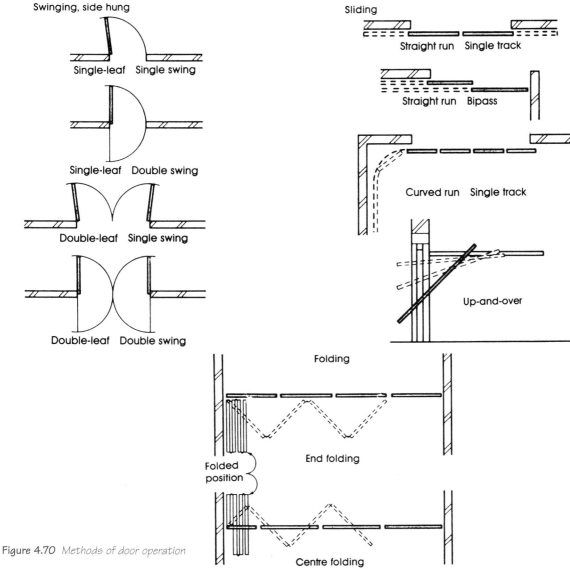

Figure 4.70 *Methods of door operation*

Manufacture of Joinery Products

Chapter 4

Swinging doors – the most common means of door operation uses side-hung doors on hinges. It is also the most suitable for pedestrian use and the most effective for weather protection, fire resistance, sound and thermal insulation.

Sliding doors are mainly used either to economise on space where it is not possible to swing a door, or for large openings that would be difficult to close off with swinging doors.

Folding doors are a combination of swinging and sliding doors. They can be used as either movable internal partitions to divide up large rooms or as doors for large warehouses and showroom entrances.

Door ironmongery

Door ironmongery is also termed **door furniture** and includes hinges, locks, latches, bolts, other security devices, handles and letter or postal plates. The hand of a door is required in order to select the correct items of ironmongery. Some locks and latches have reversible bolts, enabling either hand to be adapted to suit the situation.

Traditionally, this has always been done by viewing the door from the hinge knuckle side; if the knuckles are on the left the door is left handed, whereas if the knuckles are on the right the door is right handed. Doors may also be defined as either clockwise or anti-clockwise closing when viewed from the knuckle side. When ordering ironmongery simply stating left-hand or right-hand, clockwise or anti-clockwise can be confusing, as there may be variations between manufacturers and suppliers. The standard way now to identify handing is to use the coding in Figure 4.71.

◆ 5.0 for clockwise closing doors and indicating ironmongery fixed to the opening face (knuckle side);
◆ 5.1 for clockwise closing doors and indicating ironmongery fixed to the closing face (non-knuckle side);
◆ 6.0 for anti-clockwise closing doors and indicating ironmongery fixed to the opening face;
◆ 6.1 for anti-clockwise closing doors and indicating ironmongery fixed to the closing face.

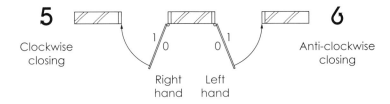

Figure 4.71 *Method for stating door handing*

Hinges

Hinges are available in a variety of materials: pressed steel is commonly used for internal doors and brass for hardwood and external doors (see Figure 4.72). Do not use steel hinges on hardwood or external doors because of rusting and subsequent staining problems. Do not use nylon, plastic or aluminium hinges on fire-resistant doors because they melt at fairly low temperatures.

Butt hinges are general purpose hinges suitable for most applications. As a general rule the leaf with the greatest number of knuckles is fixed to the door frame.

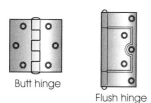
Butt hinge
Flush hinge

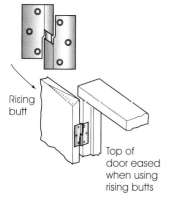
Rising butt
Top of door eased when using rising butts

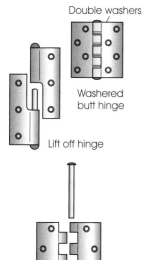
Double washers
Washered butt hinge
Lift off hinge

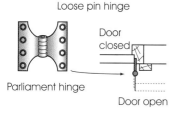
Loose pin hinge

Parliament hinge
Door closed
Door open

Figure 4.72 Range of hinges

Flush hinges can be used for the same range of purposes as a butt hinge on both cabinets and full-size room doors. They are only really suitable for lightweight doors, but they do have the advantage of easy fitting, as they do not require 'sinking in'.

Loose pin butt hinges enable easy door removal by knocking out the pins. For security reasons they should not be used for outward-opening external doors.

Lift-off butt hinges also enable easy door removal, the door being lifted off when in the open position. These are available as right- or left-handed pairs. Each pair consists of one long pin hinge, which is fitted as the lower hinge. The upper hinge has a slightly shorter pin, to aid repositioning the door.

Washered butt hinges are used for heavier doors to reduce knuckle wear and prevent squeaking.

Parliament hinges have wide leaves to extend knuckles and enable doors to fold back against the wall clearing deep architraves, etc.

Rising butts are designed to lift the door as it opens to clear obstructions such as mats and rugs. They also give a door some degree of self-closing action. In order to prevent the top edge of the door fouling in the frame as it opens and closes, the top edge must be eased. The hand of the door must be stated when ordering these items, as they cannot be reversed (i.e. they cannot be altered to suit either hand of door).

Locks, latches and other furniture
(See Figure 4.73.)

Cylinder rim latches are mainly used for entrance doors to domestic property but they provide little security on their own. When fitted, the door can be opened from the outside with the use of a key and from the inside by turning the handle. Some types have a double-locking facility, which improves their security.

Mortise deadlocks provide a straightforward key-operated locking action and is often used to provide additional security on entrance doors where cylinder rim latches are fitted. They are also used on doors where simple security is required, e.g. storerooms. The more levers a lock has the better it is, i.e. a five-lever lock provides greater security than one with three levers.

Mortise latches are used mainly for internal doors that do not require locking. The latch, which holds the door in the closed position, can be operated from either side of the door by turning the handle.

Mortise locks/latches are available in two types. The horizontal one is little used nowadays because of its length, which means that it can only be fitted to substantial doors. The vertical type is more modern and can be fitted to most types of doors. It is often known as a narrow-stile lock/latch. Both types can be used for a wide range of general-purpose doors in various locations. They are, in essence, a combination of the mortise deadlock and the mortise latch. Further variations are the Euro pattern, which uses a cylinder lock to operate the dead bolt, and bathroom privacy patterns, which use a turn button on the inside of the door.

Rebated mortise locks/latches should be used when fixing a lock/latch in double doors that have rebated stiles. The front end of this lock is cranked to fit the rebate on the stiles.

Knobsets consist of a small mortise latch and a pair of knob handles that can be locked with a key, so that they can be used as locks/latches in most situations both internally and externally. Knobsets can also be obtained without the lock in the knob for use as latches only.

Knob furniture is for use with the horizontal mortise lock/latch. It should not be used with the vertical type as hand injuries will result.

Chapter 4 Manufacture of Joinery Products

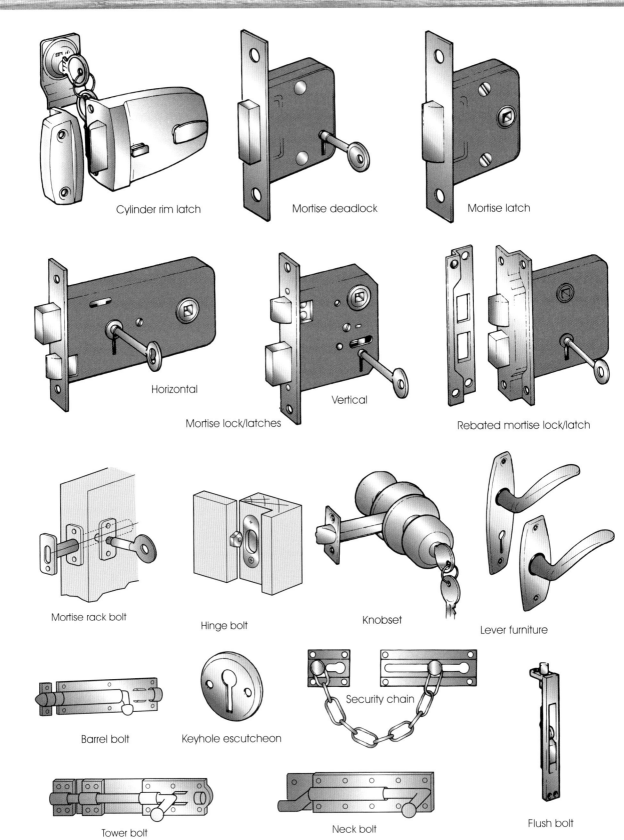

Cylinder rim latch

Mortise deadlock

Mortise latch

Horizontal

Vertical

Mortise lock/latches

Rebated mortise lock/latch

Mortise rack bolt

Hinge bolt

Knobset

Lever furniture

Barrel bolt

Keyhole escutcheon

Security chain

Tower bolt

Neck bolt

Flush bolt

Figure 4.73 *Door locks and furniture*

Keyhole escutcheon plates are used to provide a neat finish to the keyhole of both deadlocks and horizontal mortise lock/latches.

Lever furniture is available in a wide range of patterns, for use with the mortise latches and mortise lock/latches.

Barrel and tower bolts are used on external gates and doors to secure them from the inside. Two bolts are normally used, one near the top of the door and the other near the bottom. Cranked or swan neck bolts are used to secure outward opening external doors from the inside.

Flush bolts are flush fitting and therefore requires recessing into the timber. They are used for better quality work on the inside of external doors to provide additional security and also on double doors and French windows to bolt one door in the closed position. Two bolts are normally used, one at the top of the door and the other at the bottom.

Hinge bolts help to prevent a door being forced off its hinges. They provide increased security, particularly on outward opening doors where the hinge knuckle pin is vulnerable.

Mortise rack bolts are fluted key-operated dead bolts. These are mortised into the edge of the door at about 150 mm from either end.

Security chains can be fixed on front entrance doors, the slide to the door and the chain to the frame. When the chain is inserted into the slide, the door will only open a limited amount until the identity of the caller is checked.

Ironmongery positioning

Hinge positions

These are shown in Figure 4.74. Lightweight internal doors are normally hung on one pair of 75 mm hinges; glazed, half-hour fire resistant and other heavy doors need one pair of 100 mm hinges. All external doors and one-hour fire resistant doors need one-and-a-half pairs of 100 mm hinges. The standard hinge positions for flush doors are 150 mm down from the top, 225 mm up from the bottom and the third hinge where required, positioned centrally to prevent warping, or towards the top for maximum weight capacity. On panelled and glazed doors the hinges are often fixed in line with the rails to produce a more balanced look.

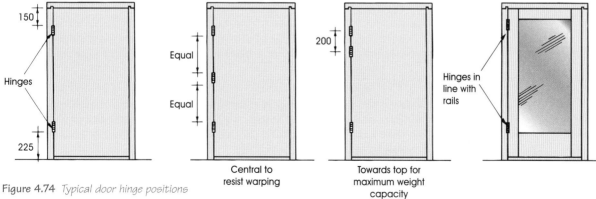

Figure 4.74 *Typical door hinge positions*

Other door furniture positions

The position of door ironmongery or furniture will depend on the type of door construction, the specification and the door manufacturer's instructions. Figure 4.75 illustrates the recommended fixing height for various items.

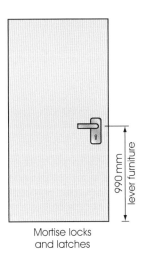

Mortise locks
and latches

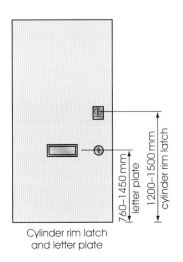

Cylinder rim latch
and letter plate

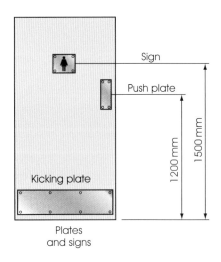

Plates
and signs

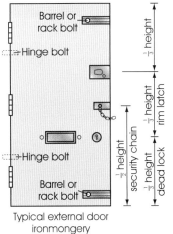

Typical external door
ironmongery

Figure 4.75 *Typical door furniture positions*

Chapter 4   Manufacture of Joinery Products

The standard position for mortise locks and latches is 990 mm from the bottom of the door to the centreline of the lever or knob furniture spindle. However, on a panelled door with a middle rail, locks/latches may be positioned centrally in the rail's width.

◆ Cylinder rim latches are positioned in the door's stile between 1200 mm and 1500 mm from the bottom of the door and the centre line of the cylinder.
◆ Before fitting any locks/latches the width of the door stile should be measured to ensure the lock/latch length is shorter than the stile's width, otherwise a narrow stile lock may be required.
◆ On external doors using both a cylinder rim latch and a mortise dead lock, the best positions for security is one-third up for the dead lock and one-third down from the top for the cylinder rim latch.
◆ Security chains are best positioned near the centre of the door in height.
◆ Hinge bolts should be positioned just below the top hinge and just above the bottom hinge.
◆ Letter plates are normally positioned centrally in a door's width and between 760 mm and 1450 mm from the bottom of the door to the centre line of the plate. Again, on panelled doors letter plates may be positioned centrally in a rail and sometimes even vertically in a stile.
◆ Information signs are normally positioned centrally in a door's width and 1500 mm from the bottom of the door to the centre of the sign.
◆ Kicking plates are fixed to the bottom face of the door for protection, keeping an even margin. Push- or finger-plates are positioned near the closing edge of a door at a height of 1200 mm to the centre of the plate. On panelled and glazed doors, they should be fixed centrally in the stile's width.

Before starting work, always read the job specification carefully as exact furniture positions may be stated. Also, read both the door manufacturer's and the ironmongery manufacturer's instructions to ensure the intended position is suitable to receive the item, e.g. the position of the lock block on a flush door, and the correct fixing procedure for a lock.

Door and ironmongery schedules

Schedules are used to record repetitive design information. Read with a range drawing and floor plans, they may be used to identify a type of door, its size, the number required, the door opening in which it fits, the hinges it will swing on and details of other furniture to be fitted to it. See Figures 4.76 to 4.79.

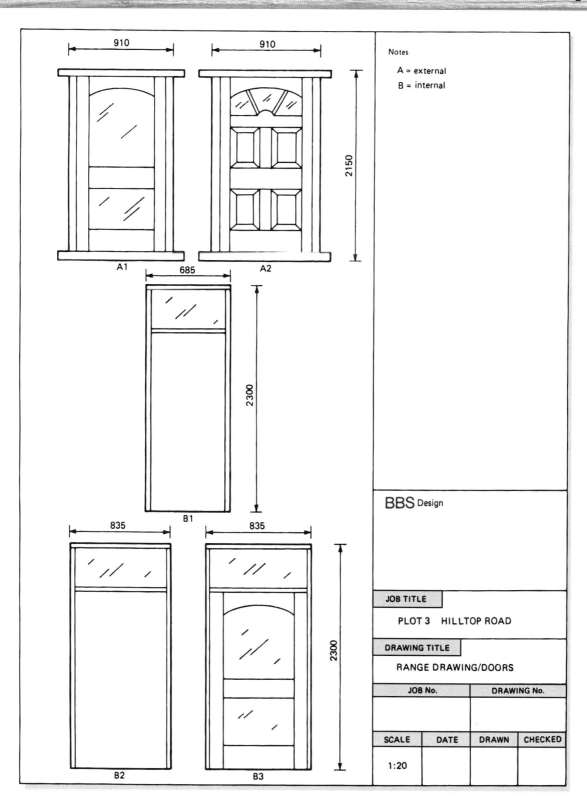

Notes

A = external
B = internal

BBS Design

JOB TITLE

PLOT 3   HILLTOP ROAD

DRAWING TITLE

RANGE DRAWING/DOORS

JOB No.		DRAWING No.	

SCALE	DATE	DRAWN	CHECKED
1:20			

Figure 4.76 *Door range drawing*

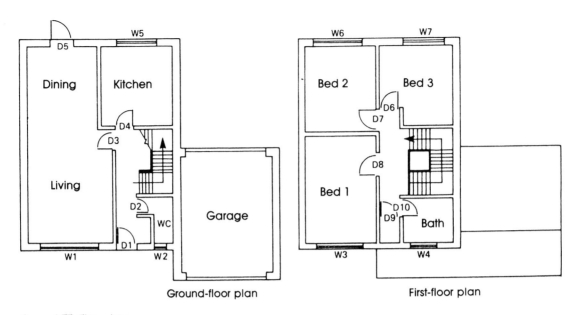

Ground-floor plan   First-floor plan

Figure 4.77 *Floor plans*

Manufacture of Joinery Products

Chapter 4

Description	D1	D2	D3	D4	D5	D6	D7	D8	D9	D10			NOTES
Type (see range)													
External glazed A1					●								
External panelled A2	●												
Internal flush B1									●				
Internal flush B2		●				●	●	●		●			
Internal glazed B3			●	●									
Size													
813 mm × 2032 mm × 44 mm	●				●								
762 mm × 1981 mm × 35 mm		●	●	●		●	●	●		●			
610 mm × 1981 mm × 35 mm									●				
Material													**BBS** DESIGN
Hardwood	●												
Softwood			●	●	●								
Plywood/polished		●											JOB TITLE
plywood/painted						●	●	●	●	●			PLOT 3 Hilltop Road
Infill													DRAWING TITLE Door Schedule/doors
6 mm tempered safety glass													JOB NO. DRAWING NO.
clear			●	●	●								
obscured	●												SCALE DATE DRAWN CHECKED

Figure 4.78 *Door schedule*

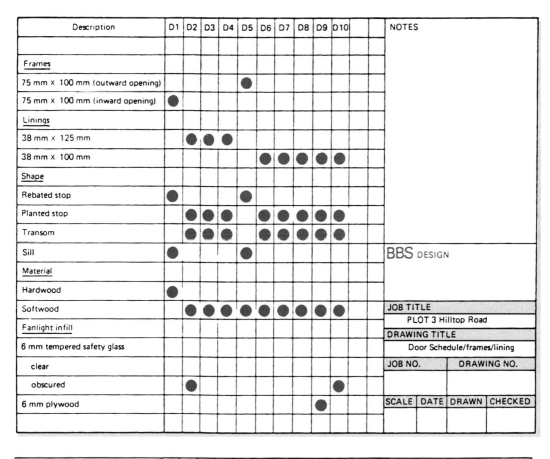

Description	D1	D2	D3	D4	D5	D6	D7	D8	D9	D10		NOTES
Frames												
75 mm × 100 mm (outward opening)					●							
75 mm × 100 mm (inward opening)	●											
Linings												
38 mm × 125 mm		●	●	●								
38 mm × 100 mm						●	●	●	●	●		
Shape												
Rebated stop	●				●							
Planted stop		●	●	●		●	●	●	●	●		
Transom		●	●	●		●	●	●	●	●		
Sill	●				●							
Material												
Hardwood	●											
Softwood		●	●	●	●	●	●	●	●	●		
Fanlight infill												
6 mm tempered safety glass												
clear												
obscured		●							●			
6 mm plywood							●					

BBS DESIGN

JOB TITLE — PLOT 3 Hilltop Road
DRAWING TITLE — Door Schedule/frames/lining
JOB NO.   DRAWING NO.
SCALE | DATE | DRAWN | CHECKED

Description	D1	D2	D3	D4	D5	D6	D7	D8	D9	D10		NOTES
Hanging												
Pair 100 mm pressed steel butt hinges			●	●	● ¹·⁵							
Pair 100 mm brass butt hinges	● ¹·⁵											
Pair 75 mm pressed steel butt hinges						●	●	●	● ¹·⁵	●		
Pair 75 mm brass butt hinges		●										
Fastening												
Rim night latch	●											
Mortise deadlock	●											
Mortise lock/latch		●			●					●		
Mortise latch			●	●		●	●	●	●			
100 mm brass bolts	● ²				● ²							
Miscellaneous												
Brass lock/latch furniture		●			●					●		
Brass latch furniture			●	●		●	●	●	●			
Brass letterplate	●											
Brass knocker	●											
Brass coat hook		● ²								● ²		
Brass escutcheon	● ²											

BBS DESIGN

JOB TITLE — PLOT 3 Hilltop Road
DRAWING TITLE — Ironmongery schedule/doors
JOB NO.   DRAWING NO.
SCALE | DATE | DRAWN | CHECKED

Figure 4.79 Door frame/lining and ironmongery schedules

Manufacture of Joinery Products

Chapter 4

Details relevant to a particular door opening are indicated in the schedules by a dot or cross. A figure is also included where more than one item is required. Extracting details from a schedule is called 'taking off'.

The following information concerning the WC door D2 has been taken off the schedules: 'One polished plywood internal flush door type B2 762 mm × 1981 mm × 35 mm, hung on one pair of 75 mm brass butts and fitted with one mortise lock/latch, one brass mortise lock/latch furniture and two brass coat hooks'.

Take off the following information from the schedules (fig 4.78 and 4.79):

◆ How many type B2 painted doors are required?
◆ Produce a list of locks and bolts required for the whole house.
◆ State the size and type of door for opening D5.

Door frames and linings

The main difference between door frames and door linings is that linings cover the full width of the reveal in which they are fixed, from wall surface to wall surface, whereas frames do not, as illustrated in Figure 4.80.

Door frames

The surround on which an external door or internal door is hung consists of a head, two jambs and, where required for external use, a threshold, normally with stuck-on solid stops rather than planted ones and of a bigger section than door linings. See Figure 4.81.

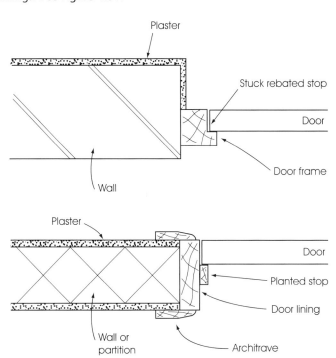

Figure 4.80 *Door frames and linings*

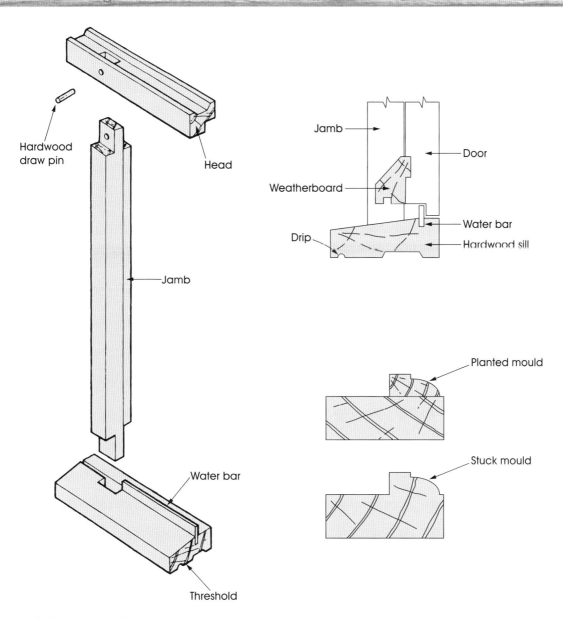

Figure 4.81 *Door frame and details*

The component parts of a door frame are jointed using draw-pinned mortise-and-tenon joints (see Figure 4.82). Draw pins are used in preference to wedges, as they will hold the joint even if the horns are cut off on-site prior to fixing. In addition, the use of draw pins has the advantage of not requiring cramps to pull up the joint during assembly. As with the assembly of window frames, by offsetting the hole in the tenon slightly towards the shoulder, the joint will be drawn up tight as the pin is driven in. The draw pin can be simply cut off flush with the frame after driving in, or it may in addition be wedged.

Storey-height frames

Figure 4.83 shows how these are used for door openings in thin non-loadbearing blockwork partitions. The jambs and head that make up the frame are grooved out on their back face to receive the building blocks. The jambs above the head are cut back to finish flush with the blockwork wall. A mortise-and-tenon joint is used between the head and the jambs (see Figure 4.84). This frame is designed to be fixed in position, at the bottom to the wall plate and at the top to the joists, before the blocks are built up (see Figure 4.85).

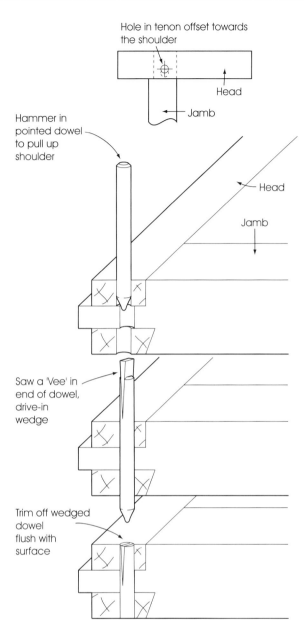

Hole in tenon offset towards the shoulder

Head

Jamb

Hammer in pointed dowel to pull up shoulder

Head

Jamb

Saw a 'Vee' in end of dowel, drive-in wedge

Trim off wedged dowel flush with surface

Figure 4.82 *Draw pinning (joint cut away to show detail)*

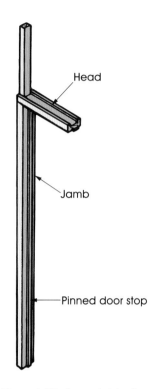

Head

Jamb

Pinned door stop

Figure 4.83 *Storey height frames*

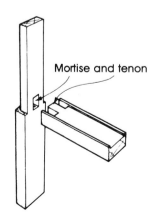

Mortise and tenon

Figure 4.84 *Joint detail (storey height frame)*

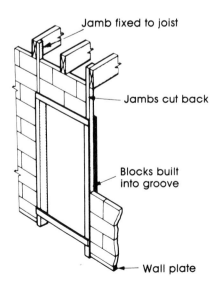

Jamb fixed to joist

Jambs cut back

Blocks built into groove

Wall plate

Figure 4.85 *Building in a storey height frame*

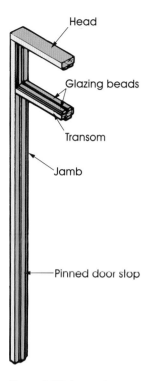

Figure 4.86 *Internal storey height frame with fanlight*

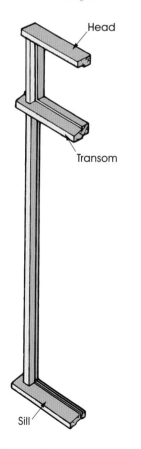

- Head
- Transom
- Sill

Figure 4.87 *External storey height frame*

Storey height frames with fanlights – Figure 4.86 shows a frame for internal use and Figure 4.87 a frame for external use. Both types consist of two jambs, a head and a transom, the external frame also has a threshold or sill.

For a plain internal frame the joint between the transom and the jamb can be a single mortise and tenon but where a rebated frame is used the joint should be a double mortise and tenon as shown in Figure 4.88.

On external storey height frames where the transom extends beyond the face, the joint will be a mortise and tenon and the overhanging edge of the transom should be housed across the face of the jambs (see Figure 4.89).

Door linings

The surrounds on which mainly internal doors are hung are normally of a thinner section than door frames.

Plain linings consist of two plain jambs and a plain head joined together using a housing or a bare-faced tongue and housing for better quality work. The planted stop is fixed around the lining after the door has been hung. (See Figure 4.90.)

Rebated linings – are used for better quality work. They consist of two rebated jambs and a rebated head. The rebate must be the correct width so that when the door is hung it finishes flush with the edges of the lining. (See Figure 4.91.)

did you know?
Rebated door linings may also be called 'casings'.

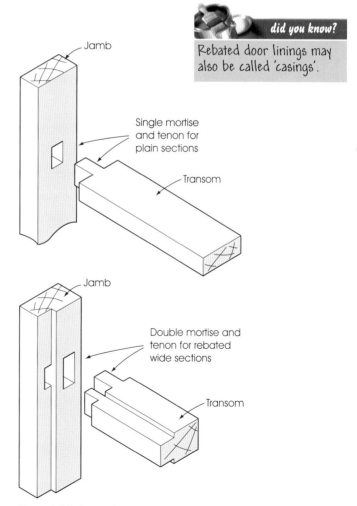

- Jamb
- Single mortise and tenon for plain sections
- Transom
- Jamb
- Double mortise and tenon for rebated wide sections
- Transom

Figure 4.88 *Internal storey height transom joints for frames with fanlights*

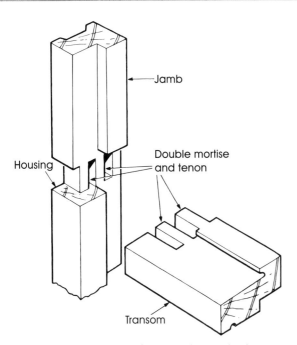

Figure 4.89 *Transom joint for external storey height frame with fanlight*

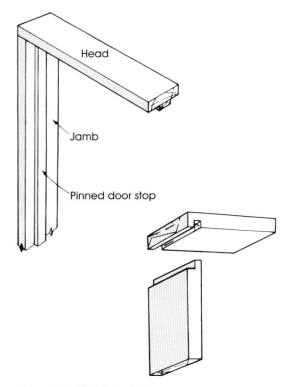

Figure 4.90 *Plain lining joint*

Skeleton linings are used for deeper reveals, where the brickwork is too thick for a normal lining to be used. They consist of a basic framework, which is stub tenoned together. A stopped bare-faced tongue and housing is used between the head and the jambs. A ply or solid timber lining is used to cover the framework and form the rebate to receive the door. (See Figure 4.92.)

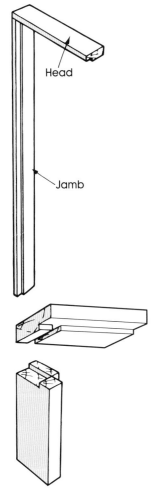

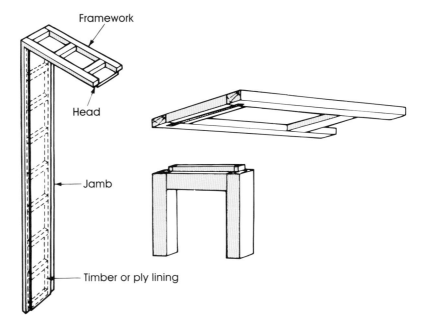

Figure 4.91 *Rebated lining joint*　　　　**Figure 4.92** *Skeleton lining joint*

Assembly of door frames and linings

It is standard practice to assemble door frames in the joiners shop, whereas linings are normally sent to site in flat-pack form, to be assembled by the carpenter.

Frames without a threshold are assembled with a temporary distance piece and braces to hold the jambs parallel and square. Frames with a threshold may be assembled with temporary braces for squaring purposes. Both are illustrated in Figure 4.93.

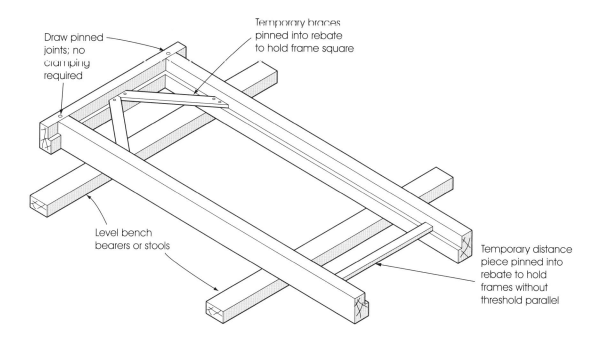

Draw pinned joints; no clamping required

Temporary braces pinned into rebate to hold frame square

Level bench bearers or stools

Temporary distance piece pinned into rebate to hold frames without threshold parallel

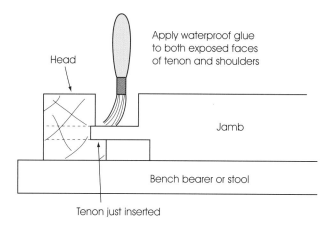

Apply waterproof glue to both exposed faces of tenon and shoulders

Head

Jamb

Bench bearer or stool

Tenon just inserted

Figure 4.93 *Door frame assembly*

Door sets

A door set consists of a pre-hung door and frame or lining, complete with all ironmongery. Architraves are normally fixed to one side of the set and loose pinned on the other. All work is undertaken in the joinery shop and supplied to site ready for fixing into its opening. The main advantages of using door sets is the 'joiners shop quality' and the considerable saving in on-site time to install. See Figure 4.94.

Door hanging

Speed and confidence in door hanging can be achieved by following the procedure illustrated in Figure 4.95 and outlined below:

◆ Measure height and width of door opening.
◆ Locate and mark the top and hanging side of the opening and door.
◆ Cut off the horns.
◆ 'Shoot' (plane to fit) in the hanging stile of door to fit the hanging side of the opening. A leading edge will be required to prevent binding.

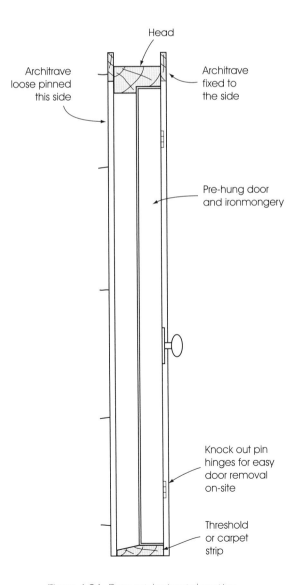

Figure 4.94 *Door set horizontal section*

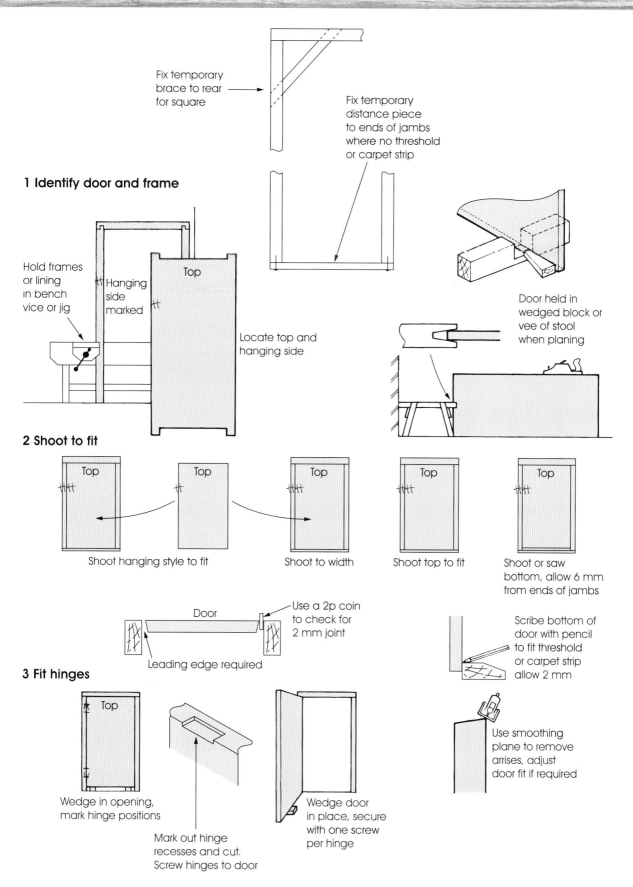

Figure 4.95 *Typical door-hanging procedure*

did you know?

Arrises are sharp corners. They should be removed from joinery to soften the corner and provide a better surface for a subsequent paint or polish finish.

♦ 'Shoot' the door to width. Allow a 2 mm joint all around between door and frame or lining. Use a 2p coin to check. The closing side will require planing to a slight angle to allow it to close.

♦ 'Shoot' the top of the door (if required) to fit the head of the opening; allow a 2 mm joint. Saw or shoot the bottom of the door (if required) to give a 6 mm gap at floor level or a 2 mm gap at a threshold.

♦ Mark out and cut in the hinges. Screw one leaf of each hinge to the door.

♦ Offer up the door to the opening and screw the other leaf of each hinge to the frame.

♦ Adjust fit as required. Remove all arrises (sharp edges) to soften the corners and provide a better surface for the subsequent paint finish. If the closing edge rubs the frame, the hinges may be proud and require the recesses to be cut deeper. If the recesses are too deep, the door will not close fully and will tend to spring open, which is known as 'hinge bound'. In this case a thin cardboard strip can be placed in the recess to pack out the hinge.

♦ Fit and fix the lock.

♦ Fit any other ironmongery, e.g. bolts, letter plates, handles.

Mortise deadlock, latch or lock/latch

The fitting procedure is shown in Figure 4.96.

Always consult manufacturers' instructions before starting.

1. Use the lock as a guide to mark the mortise position on the door edge at the pre-marked height.
2. Set a marking gauge to half the thickness of the door. Score a centre line down the mortise position to mark for drilling.
3. Select a drill bit the same diameter as the thickness of the lock body. An oversize bit will weaken the door; use an undersize one and additional paring will be required. A hand brace and bit or power drill and spade bit may be used. Mark the required drilling depth on the bit using a piece

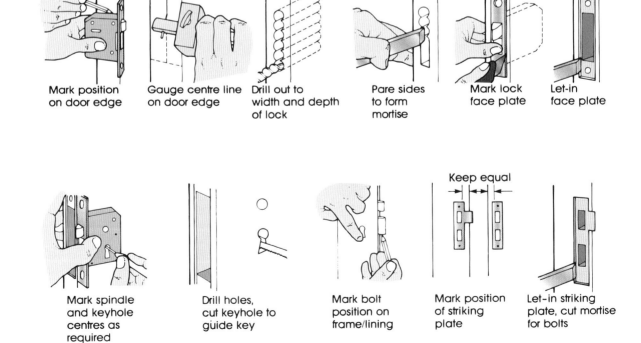

Figure 4.96 *Fitting procedure for locks and latches*

did you know?

When using brass or other soft screw to fix ironmongery, a steel screw should be inserted first, to cut a thread, and then it should be replaced with the softer screw. Failure to do this may result not only in screw head damage but it may even snap off when being screwed in.

of masking tape. Drilling too deep will again weaken the door as well as increase the risk in panel and glazed doors of the drill breaking out right through the stile.

4. Working from the top, drill out the mortise, with each hole slightly overlapping the one before.
5. Use a chisel to pare away waste between holes to form a neat rectangular mortise.
6. Slide the lock into the mortise and mark around the faceplate.
7. Remove the lock and use a marking gauge to score deeper lines along the grain, as this helps to prevent the fine edge breaking out or splitting when chiselling out the housing.
8. Use a chisel to form the housing for the faceplate (let in). The surface can first be feathered (as when recessing hinges) and finally cleaned.
9. Hold the lock against the face of the door, with the faceplate flush with the door edge and lined up with the faceplate housing. Mark the centre positions of the spindle and keyhole as required with a bradawl.
10. Use a 16 mm drill bit to drill the spindle hole, working from both sides to avoid breakout, or clamp a waste piece to the back of the door.
11. Use a 10 mm drill bit to drill the keyhole, again working from both sides. Cut the key slot with a padsaw and clean out with a chisel to form a key guide. Alternatively, use a 6 mm drill bit to drill out a second hole below the 10 mm hole and chisel out waste to form a key guide. Never drill a larger hole for the key as it will not give a guide when inserting the key, making it a hit-and-miss affair.
12. Insert the lock, and check the spindle and keyholes align from both sides. Secure the faceplate with screws. Re-check that the key works.
13. With the dead bolt out, close the door against the frame and mark the bolt and latch positions on the edge of the frame. Square these positions across the face of the frame.
14. Set the adjustable square from the face of the door to the front edge of the latch or dead bolt. Use it to mark the position on the face of the frame.
15. Hold the striking plate over the latch or dead bolt position and mark around the striking plate. Gauge vertical lines to prevent breakout when chiselling.
16. Chisel out to let in the striking plate. Again, you may find it easier to feather first before finally cleaning out. The extended lead-in or lip for the latch may require a slightly deeper bevelled housing or recess.
17. Check for fit and screw the striking plate in place. Select a chisel slightly smaller than the striking plate bolt-holes.
18. Chop mortises to accommodate both the latch and dead bolt. Some striking plates have boxed bolt-holes. These must be cut beforehand.
19. Finally, fit the lever furniture, knob furniture or keyhole escutcheon plates as appropriate and check for smooth operation. When fixing keyhole escutcheon plates, the key should be passed through the plate and into the lock and centralised on the key shaft before screwing.

Cylinder rim latch

The fitting procedure is shown in Figure 4.97.

Always consult manufacturer's instructions:

1. Use the template supplied with the lock at the pre-marked height to mark the centre of the cylinder hole.
2. Use a 32 mm auger bit in a brace or a spade bit in a power drill to drill the cylinder hole. Drill from one side until the point just protrudes. Complete the hole from the other side to make a neat hole, avoiding breakout, or alternatively by cramping a block to the door.
3. Pass the cylinder through the hole from the outside face and secure it to the mounting plate on the inside with the connecting machine screws.
4. Ensure that the cylinder key slot is vertical before fully tightening the screws. For some thinner doors these machine screws may require shortening with a

hacksaw before use. If required, secure the mounting plate to the door with woodscrews.

5. Check the projection of the flat connection strip. This operates the latch and is designed to be cut to suit the door thickness. If necessary use a hacksaw to trim the strip so that it projects about 15 mm past the mounting plate.

6. Align the arrows on the backplate of the rim lock and the turnable thimble.

7. Place the rim lock case over the mounting plate ensuring that the connection strip enters the thimble.

8. Mark out and let in the rim lock lip in the edge of the door if required.

9. Secure the rim lock case to the door or mounting plate with wood or machine screws as required. Check both the key and inside handle for smooth operation.

10. Close the door and use the rim lock case to mark the position of the keep (striking plate) on the edge of the door frame.

11. Open the door and use the keep to mark the lip recess on the face of the frame. Chisel out a recess to accommodate the keep's lip. Secure the keep to the frame using woodscrews.

12. Finally check from both sides to ensure a smooth operation.

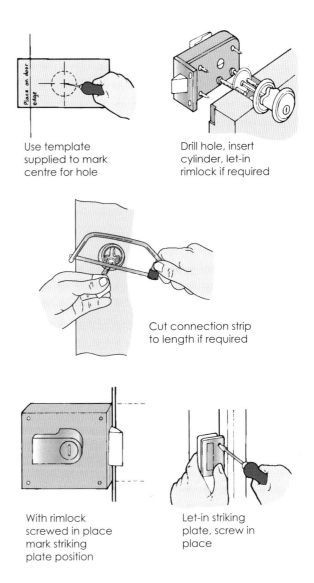

Use template supplied to mark centre for hole

Drill hole, insert cylinder, let-in rimlock if required

Cut connection strip to length if required

With rimlock screwed in place mark striking plate position

Let-in striking plate, screw in place

Figure 4.97 *Fixing a cylinder rim night latch*

Letter plate

The fitting procedure is shown in Figure 4.98.

Always consult manufacturers' instructions.

1. Mark the centreline of the plate on the face of the door.
2. Position the plate over the centreline and mark around it.
3. Measure the size of the opening flap and mark the cut-out on the door. Allow about 2 mm larger than the flap, to ensure ease of operation.
4. Mark the position of the holes for the securing bolts.
5. Cramp an off-cut of timber to the back of the door to prevent damage from drill breakout. Alternatively, the holes can be drilled from both sides.
6. Drill holes for the fixing bolts and at each corner of the flap cut-out.
7. Use a jigsaw or padsaw to saw from hole to hole.
8. Neaten up the cut-out if required using glass paper. Remove the arris from the inside edges.
9. Position the letter plate and secure, using the fixing bolts.
10. Check the flap for ease of operation and adjust if required.

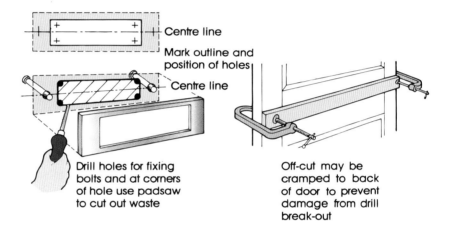

Figure 4.98 *Fitting procedure for a letter plate*

Tower and barrel bolts

The fitting procedure is shown in Figure 4.99.

Always consult manufacturers' instructions.

1. Place the bolt in the required position. Mark one of the screw holes through the backplate with a bradawl or pilot drill.
2. Insert a screw, ensuring the bolt is parallel or square to the edge of the door, and insert a screw at the other end of the bolt.
3. Fix keep plate centrally, over drilled hole. This may be let in or surface.
4. Move the bolt to the locked position and slide the keep over the bolt.
5. Mark the screw holes in the keep and screw in place.
6. Check the bolt works smoothly before inserting the remaining screws.

Cranked or swan necked bolts will require a hole drilling in the head of the door frame to receive the bolt:

1. Position and secure the bolt as before.
2. Slide the bolt to the locked position and mark around the bolt. Use an auger bit slightly larger than the width of the bolt to drill a hole in the marked position. Ensure the bolt can slide to its full length.
3. Check for smooth operation.

Manufacture of Joinery Products

Chapter 4

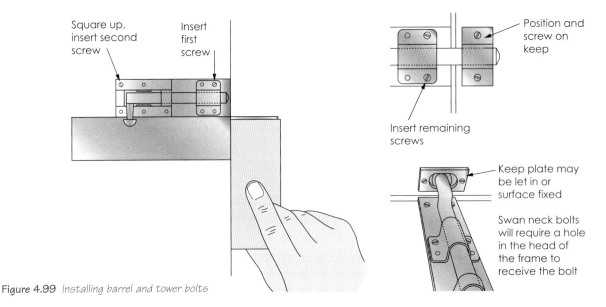

Figure 4.99 *Installing barrel and tower bolts*

Mortise rack bolt

The fitting procedure is shown in Figure 4.100.

Always consult manufacturers' instructions.

1. Use a marking gauge to score a centreline on the edge of the door.
2. Mark the centre of the bolt hole using a try square and pencil. Transfer the line onto the face of the door that the bolt will operate from.
3. Select an auger or spade bit slightly larger than the bolt barrel. Drill a hole in the edge of the door. Use a piece of tape wrapped around the bit as a depth guide.
4. Insert the bolt, and then turn the faceplate so that it is parallel to the door edge. Mark around the faceplate with a pencil.
5. Remove the bolt, then gauge the parallel edges and, using a sharp chisel, 'let in' the faceplate.
6. Place the bolt on the face of the door. Use the bradawl to mark the key position.
7. Use a 10 mm bit to drill the keyhole through the face of the door, into the bolt hole.
8. Insert the bolt into the hole, then check that the faceplate finishes flush and that the keyhole lines up. Insert the fixing screws.
9. Insert the key through the keyhole plate into the bolt. Position the keyhole plate centrally over the key and insert the fixing screws.
10. Close the door and turn the key to rack the bolt to its locked position. The point on the bolt will mark the clearance hole centre position on the frame.
11. Drill the clearance hole for the bolt in the frame on the marked centre.
12. Close the door. Rack the bolt and check for the correct alignment of the bolt clearance hole.
13. 'Let in' the keep centrally over the clearance hole and insert the fixing screws.
14. Check for smooth operation.

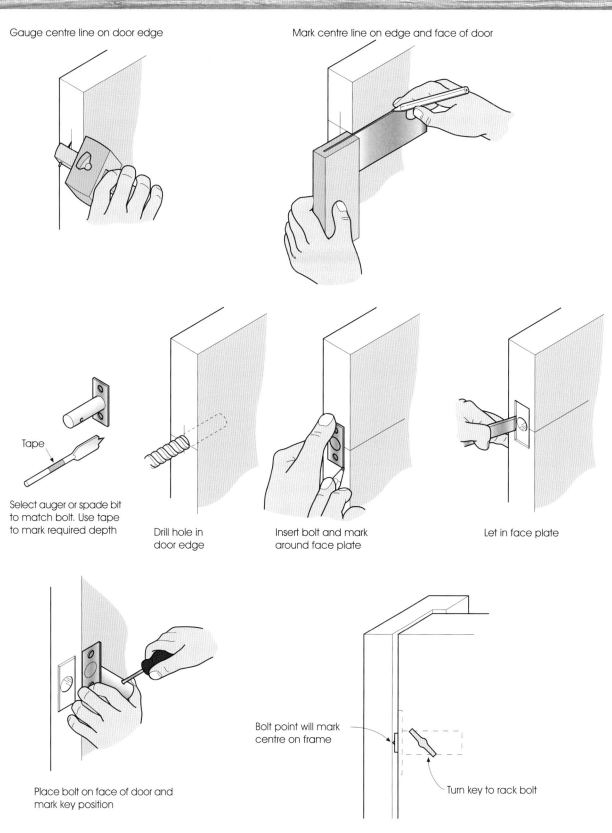

Gauge centre line on door edge

Mark centre line on edge and face of door

Tape

Select auger or spade bit to match bolt. Use tape to mark required depth

Drill hole in door edge

Insert bolt and mark around face plate

Let in face plate

Place bolt on face of door and mark key position

Bolt point will mark centre on frame

Turn key to rack bolt

Figure 4.100 Installing a mortise rack bolt

Fixing architrave

Architrave is the decorative trim that is placed internally around door openings to mask the joint between wall and timber and to conceal any subsequent shrinkage and expansion.

Figure 4.101 shows that a set of architraves consist of a horizontal head and two vertical jambs or legs. A 6 mm to 9 mm margin is normally left between the frame or lining edge and the architrave (see Figure 4.102). This margin provides a neat appearance to an opening: an unsightly joint line would result if architraves were kept flush with the edge of the opening.

The return corners of a set of architraves are mitred. For right-angled returns (90 degrees) the mitre will be 45 degrees (half the total angle) and can be cut using a mitre box or block as shown in Figure 4.103.

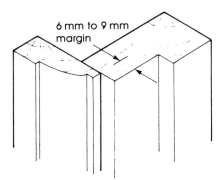

Figure 4.102 *Margin to architraves*

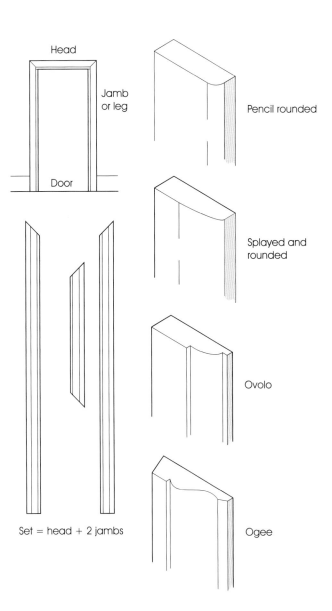

Head

Jamb or leg

Door

Set = head + 2 jambs

Pencil rounded

Splayed and rounded

Ovolo

Ogee

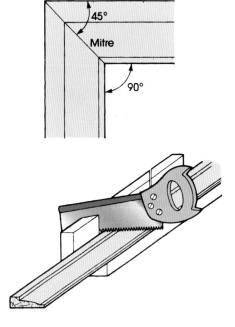

Manufacture of Joinery Products

Chapter 4

Figure 4.101 *Architrave*

Figure 4.103 *Mitre to architraves*

Mitres for corners other than right angles will be half the angle of intersection. They can be practically found by marking the outline of the intersecting trim on the frame/lining or wall, and joining the inside and outside corners to give the mitre line (see Figure 4.104). Mouldings can be marked directly from this or alternatively an adjustable bevel can be set up for use.

The head is normally marked, cut and temporarily fixed in position first as shown in Figure 4.105. The jambs can then be marked, cut, eased if required and subsequently fixed.

Where the corner is not square or you have been less than accurate in cutting the mitre, it will require easing, either with a block plane or by running a tenon saw through the mitre.

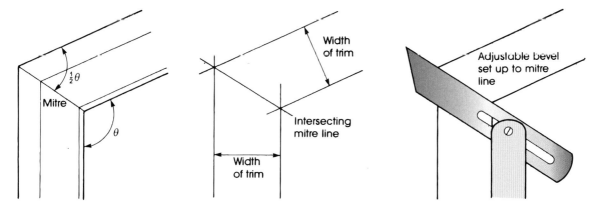

Figure 4.104 *Determining mitre for corners other than right angles*

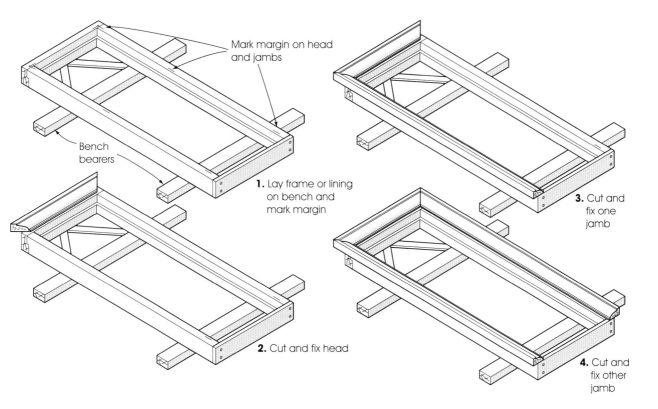

Figure 4.105 *Marking and fixing architraves*

Manufacture of Joinery Products

Chapter 4

Fixing is normally direct to the door frame/lining at between 200 mm and 300 mm centres using typically 38 mm or 50 mm long oval or lost-head nails. These should be positioned in the fillets or quirks (flat surface or groove in moulding) and punched in (see Figure 4.106).

Mitres should be nailed through their top edge to reinforce the joint and ensure both faces are kept flush (see Figure 4.107); 38 mm oval or lost-head nails are suitable for this purpose.

Plinth block A plinth block was traditionally fixed at the base of an architrave to take the knocks and abrasions at floor level (see Figure 4.108). It is also used to ease fixing problems that occur when skirtings are thicker than the architrave.

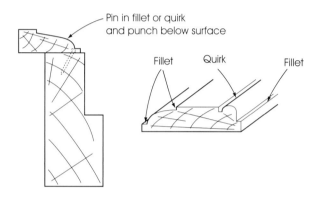

Figure 4.106 *Fixing architraves*

Figure 4.107 *Nailing mitre joints at corners of architraves*

In current practice plinth blocks will rarely be found except in restoration work, in new high-quality work in traditional style or where the skirting is thicker than the architrave.

Architraves may be butt jointed to the plinth block, but traditionally they were joined using bare-faced tenon and screws as illustrated in Figure 4.109.

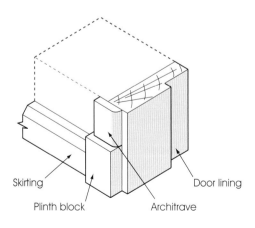

Figure 4.108 *Use of a plinth block*

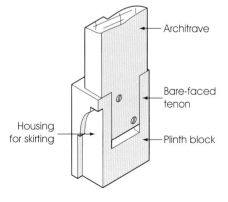

Figure 4.109 *Traditional jointing of architrave plinth block (rear view)*

11. Name and sketch the joint that is used between the stile and the middle/ bottom rails of a framed, ledged and braced door.

12. State the purpose of door and ironmongery schedules.

13. Produce a sketch to show the typical positions of the hinges and mortise lock/ latch to an external plywood flush door.

14. State why manufacturer's instructions should be followed when fitting ironmongery.

15. Define 'arris' and state why it should be removed from joinery.

16. Explain the treatment required to the top edge of a door head when hung using rising butts.

17. List the sequence of operations for hanging a door in a joiners shop as part of a door set.

18. Braces are incorporated into matchboarded doors in order to:
    (a) provide a fixing for the hinges
    (b) prevent the door from sagging
    (c) joint matchboarding together
    (d) protect the door from weather.

19. Produce a sketch to show the jointing arrangement between the jamb and head of a rebated door lining.

20. Describe a situation where architrave plinth blocks may be specified.

Stairs

A stairway can be defined as a series of steps (combination of tread and riser) giving floor-to-floor access. Each continuous set of steps is called a **flight**. **Landings** are introduced between floor levels either to break up a long flight, giving a rest point, or to change the direction of the stair.

Straight flight stairs

These run in one direction for the entire length. Figure 4.110 shows there are three different variations.

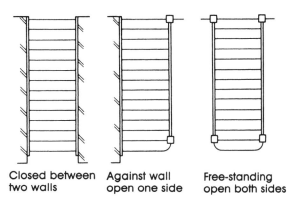

| Closed between two walls | Against wall open one side | Free-standing open both sides |

Figure 4.110 *Straight flight stairs*

The flight that is closed between two walls (also known as a cottage stair) is the simplest and most economical to make. Its handrail is usually a simple section fixed either directly on to the wall or on brackets.

The flight fixed against one wall is said to be open on one side. This open or outer string is normally terminated and supported at either end by a newel post. A balustrade must be fixed to this side to provide protection. The infilling of this can be either open or closed and is usually capped by a handrail. Where the width of the flight exceeds 1 m, a wall handrail will also be required.

Where the flight is freestanding, neither side being against a wall, it is said to be open both sides. The open sides are treated in the same way as the previous flight.

Stair construction

The four main methods of constructing straight flight stairs are illustrated in Figure 4.111.

◆ Close string: having parallel strings with the treads and risers being housed into their faces and secured by gluing and wedging.
◆ Cut string: having one or more strings that have been cut to conform to the tread and riser profile. Treads sit on the strings' horizontal cut portion and the risers are mitred to the vertical portion.
◆ Open riser: stairs with no risers, also termed open plan stairs. Treads are either housed or mortised into the strings. Infilling to the balustrade is often range style planks screwed to the face of the newels.
◆ Alternating tread: a narrow steeply pitched form of open riser stair used for access to a loft conversion in a domestic property, where there is insufficient space to accommodate a full-size stair.

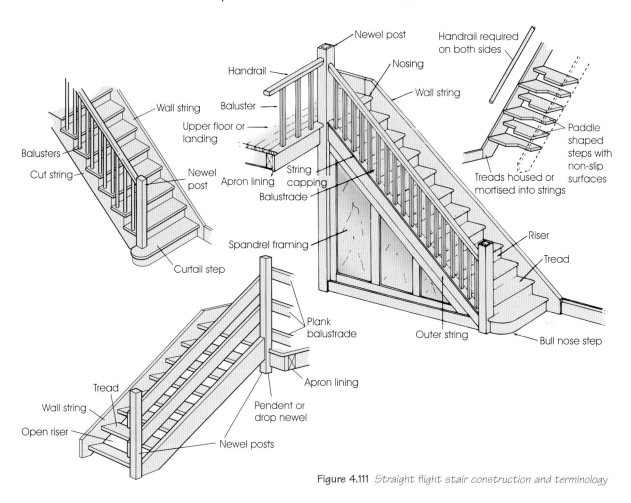

Figure 4.111 *Straight flight stair construction and terminology*

Manufacture of Joinery Products

Chapter 4

Stair terminology

Apron lining – the boards used to finish the edge of a trimmed opening in the floor.

Balustrade – the handrail and the infilling between it and the string, landing or floor. This can be called either an open or closed balustrade, depending on the infilling.

Baluster – the short vertical infilling members of an open balustrade.

Bull nose step – the quarter-rounded end step at the bottom of a flight of stairs.

Carriage – a raking timber fixed under wide stairs to support the centre of the treads and risers. Brackets are fixed to the side of the carriage to provide further support across the width of the treads.

Commode step – a step with a curved tread and riser normally occurring at the bottom of a flight.

Curtail step – the half-rounded or scroll-end step at the bottom of a flight.

Newel – the large sectioned vertical member at each end of the string. Where an upper newel does not continue down to the floor level below it is known as a pendant or drop newel.

Nosing – the front edge of a tread or the finish to the floorboards around a stairwell opening.

Riser – the vertical member of a step.

Spandrel – the triangular area formed under the stairs. This can be left open or closed in with spandrel framing to form a cupboard.

String – the board into which the treads and risers are housed or cut. They are also named according to their type, for example, wall string, outer string, close string, cut string and wreathed string.

Tread – the horizontal member of a step. It can be called a parallel tread or a tapered tread, etc. depending on its shape.

Stair regulations

The design and construction of stairs is closely controlled by the Building Regulations. These set out different requirements for stairs, depending on the use of the building in which they are located. Table 4.1 summarizes these requirements.

Table 4.1 *Stair requirements (Building Regulations)*

Requirement	Types of building where stairs are located		
	Private: stairs for domestic use in a dwelling occupied by a single household	Institutional and assembly: stairs serving places where a substantial number of people gather	Other: stairs serving all other buildings
Pitch	Maximum of 42°	Governed by tread and riser requirements	

Pitch

Table 4.1 continued ...

Requirement	Types of building where stairs are located		
Number of risers	Good practice not to exceed 16 without an intermediate landing. Consecutive flights of more than 36 risers must change direction between flights by at least 30°	Maximum of 16 for assembly buildings. Consecutive flights of more than 36 risers must change direction between flights by at least 30°	Maximum of 16 for shops. Consecutive flights of more than 36 risers must change direction between flights by at least 30°
Rise of step	Maximum of 220 mm	Maximum of 180 mm	Maximum of 190 mm
Going of step	Minimum of 220 mm (note: maximum rise cannot be used with minimum going as it will be over the pitch requirement)	Minimum of 280 mm. May be reduced to 250 mm if the floor area served by the stair is less than 100 m²	Minimum of 250 mm
Combined rise and going	Twice the rise plus the going 2R + G to fall between 550 mm and 700 mm		
Width of stair	No minimum requirement. Except when used as a means of escape, then the minimum width is determined by the number of people assessed as using the stair in an emergency: up to 50 people minimum width of 800 mm; 51 to 150 people minimum width of 1000 mm; 151 to 220 people minimum width of 1100 mm. Minimum widths for over 220 people depend of whether there is to be a phased or simultaneous evacuation (see Building Regulations for calculation formula). In all cases stairs for the disabled, where there is not a lift, must be a minimum of 1000 mm between handrails		

Number of risers diagram: Landing — Landing — Up — Max 16 risers per flight — Max 36 risers before change of direction — At least 30°

Rise of step diagram: Rise — Top of tread to top of tread

Going of step diagram: Going — Nosing to nosing — Going — Face of riser to face of riser

Combined rise and going diagram:
R = 200 mm
G = 275 mm
2R+G = 675 mm
OK for private use

Width of stair diagram: Wall to handrail — Handrail to handrail — Wall to handrail on balustrade — Minor projections ignored

Table 4.1 continued ...

Requirement	Types of building where stairs are located
Headroom stair 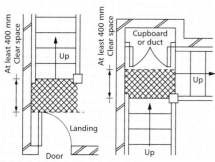	Minimum of 2 m. May be reduced for loft conversions in private dwellings
Headroom landing	Minimum of 2 m. May be reduced for loft conversions in private dwellings
Landings 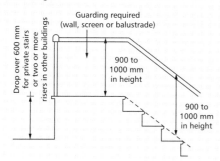	Must be provided at the top and bottom of every flight. The length and width of landings must be at least the width of the stair; part of the floor may count as a landing. Landing must be free from permanent obstructions. A door may swing over the landing at the bottom of a flight, but must leave a clear space of 400 mm across the full width of the flight. Doors to cupboards and ducts may open in a similar way over landings at the top of a flight
Guarding	Guarding in the form of a wall screen or balustrade is required to protect the sides of flights and landings in all buildings. Guarding need not be provided in private dwellings where the drop is 600 mm or less, or in other buildings where there are fewer than two risers. In buildings likely to be used by children under 5 years old, this guarding should not be easily climbed or permit the passage of a 100 mm sphere. Heights for all buildings are the same as for handrails, between 900 mm and 1000 mm measured vertically from the pitch line or floor to the top

Table 4.1 continued ...

Requirement	Types of building where stairs are located

Handrail

Handrail height and provision

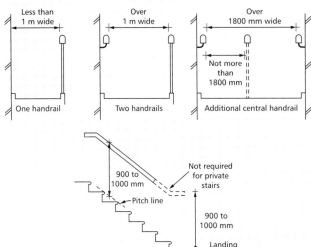

Less than 1 m wide — One handrail

Over 1 m wide — Two handrails

Over 1800 mm wide — Additional central handrail

Not more than 1800 mm

900 to 1000 mm — Pitch line

Not required for private stairs

900 to 1000 mm — Landing floor

Handrail required on one side of stair if under 1 m wide, and on both sides if over 1 m. Height for all handrails should be between 900 mm and 1000 mm measured vertically above the pitch line or landing to the top of the rail. Stairways in public buildings over 1800 mm wide should be subdivided by a handrail so that subdivisions so not exceed 1800 mm. Handrails are not required over the bottom two steps in private stairs, except when intended for disabled use

Balustrading

Balustrading

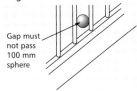

Gap must not pass 100 mm sphere

Balustrading can be used to form the required guarding to the sides of flights and landings. Again, in buildings likely to be used by children under 5 years old, the balustrade should not be easily climbed or permit the passage of a 100 mm sphere

Open riser stairs

Open riser stairs

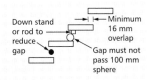

Down stand or rod to reduce gap

Minimum 16 mm overlap

Gap must not pass 100 mm sphere

Open risers permitted, but for safety the treads should overlap by at least 16 mm. In all stairways that are likely to be used by children under 5 years old, the gap between treads must not permit the passage of a 100 mm sphere

Tapered tread stairs

Tapered tread stairs

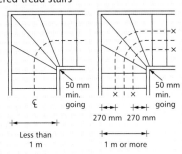

50 mm min. going — Less than 1 m

50 mm min. going — 270 mm 270 mm — 1 m or more

The minimum going at any part of the tread within the width of the stair should not be less than 50 mm. The going is measured on the centre line of the stairs if they are not more than 1 m wide or at points 270 mm in from the ends of the treads for wider stairs. All consecutive treads should have the same taper. Where stairs contain both tapered and parallel treads, the going of the tapered treads should not be less than the parallel ones

Table 4.1 continued ...

Requirement	Types of building where stairs are located
Stairs to loft conversions Stairs to loft conversions 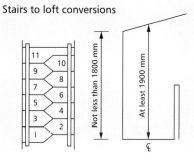	Alternating tread may be permitted for loft conversions where there is no room for a proper staircase. They can only be used to give access to one room, and must have handrails on both sides and non-slip treads. Headroom may be reduced if the height at the centre of the stair is at least 1900 mm and not less than 1800 mm at the side

Stair construction and assembly

The construction of any staircase with closed strings follows the same basic procedure, with slight variations depending on the particular type of stair.

The housings in the string can be cut out on a CNC machine or by using a portable router and a stair housing template (see Figure 4.112). Where neither of these is available, they can be cut by hand using the sequence of operations shown in Figure 4.113.

1. Bore out at nosing end with brace and bit.
2. Clean out nosing and cut edges of housing with a tenon saw.
3. Clean out waste with a chisel and hand router.

A method of forming a bull-nose step is shown in Figure 4.114. The curved section of the riser is reduced to a 2 mm thickness and bent around a laminated block. The wedges tighten the riser around the block and hold it there until the glue has set. The reduced section of the riser should be steamed before bending. It can then be bent around the block fairly easily without risk of breaking. As an alternative to the use of solid timber, the rise of a bull-nose step may be formed using bendy plywood around the laminated block. Splayed end steps are sometimes used in cheaper quality work with the riser mitred and tongued at the joints (see Figure 4.115).

Figure 4.116 shows three alternatives for tread and riser details. The tread can be made from 25 mm timber and the riser traditionally from 19 mm timber or, as is now standard practice, 9 mm or 12 mm plywood is used for the risers.

Figure 4.117 shows how each step (tread and riser) is made up in a jig before being fixed to the strings. Glue blocks strengthen the joint between the tread and the riser. The absence or loosening of these often results in squeaky stairs.

A part view of the steps fixed into a string is illustrated in 4.118. The treads and risers are glued and securely wedged into their positions in the string housing.

Manufacture of Joinery Products

Chapter 4

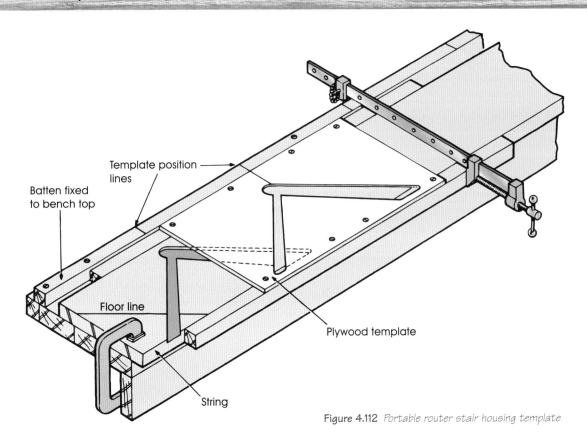

Template position lines

Batten fixed to bench top

Floor line

String

Plywood template

Figure 4.112 *Portable router stair housing template*

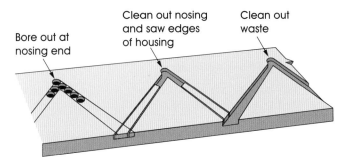

Bore out at nosing end

Clean out nosing and saw edges of housing

Clean out waste

Figure 4.113 *Sequence of operations*

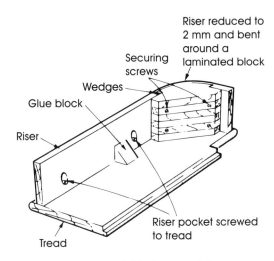

Riser reduced to 2 mm and bent around a laminated block

Securing screws

Wedges

Glue block

Riser

Tread

Riser pocket screwed to tread

Figure 4.114 *Forming a bull-nose step*

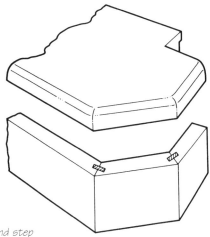

Figure 4.115 *Splayed end step*

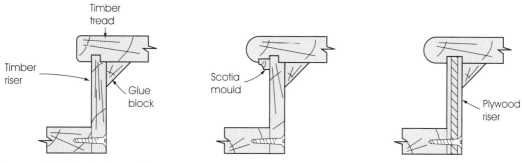

Figure 4.116 *Tread and riser details*

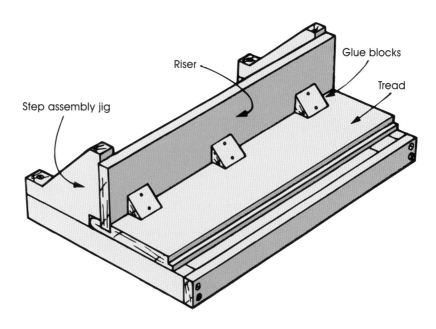

Figure 4.117 *Step assembly jig*

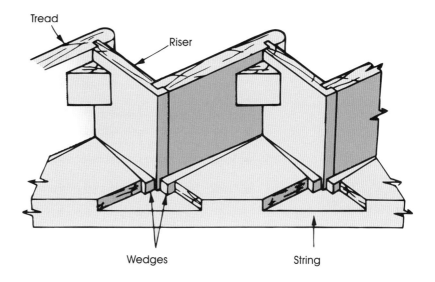

Figure 4.118
Fixing of steps into string

Where the stairs are open on one side, the outer string and handrail will be mortised at both ends into newel posts (see Figure 4.119). The newels will also require housing out to receive the treads and risers as illustrated in Figure 4.120.

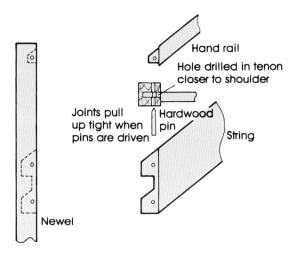

Figure 4.119 *String and handrail to newel joints*

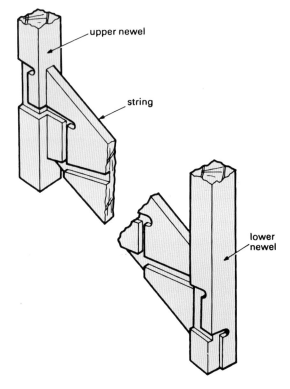

Figure 4.120 *Housing out newels*

Assembly of close string stairs

The on-edge assembly method employs a cramping jig to cramp up the strings and hold the staircase square. The following procedure is illustrated in Figure 4.121.

◆ Clean up the inner housed faces of the string, the upper face and edge of tread and exposed face of the risers.
◆ Pre-assemble the treads and risers including glue blocks.
◆ Position one string on base of the cramping up frame.
◆ Apply glue to the string housings and tread riser intersections of the pre-assembled steps. Place the steps in position.
◆ Apply glue to the housings of the other string and place in position over the steps.
◆ Close the cramping frame and tap up all the treads and risers, making sure they are all fully home in their housings.
◆ Glue and drive the wedges for the treads. Trim off any surplus length, with a chisel, so that they clear the riser housings.
◆ Glue and drive the wedges for the risers.
◆ Screw bottom edge of risers to back edge of treads at about 225 mm centres.
◆ Temporarily brace underside of stair, with diagonal braces or a piece of sheet material to prevent it raking out of square before installation.
◆ Finally, remove any squeezed-out surplus glue from seen faces with a damp cloth. Clean up outer face and top edge of string. Remove any sharp arrises.
◆ It is normal practice to assemble the flight of stairs to this stage only, for ease of handling and installation. Each flight will be separate, with the bottom bullnose step, top nosing, newels, handrail and balustrade supplied loose, ready for on-site completion.

1. Place pre-assembled step in string

2. Place other string over steps

3. Close jig and tap up steps in housings

Mechanically operated beam

Proprietary cramping jig

Spreader beam

Angle frame

Folding wedges

Angled frame jig bolted to bench

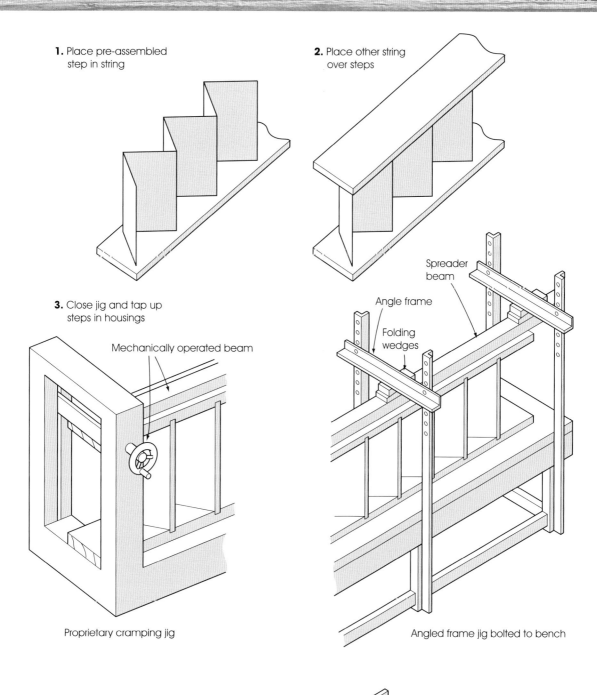

4. Wedge up, screw and brace underside

Piece of plywood fixed to underside to prevent raking

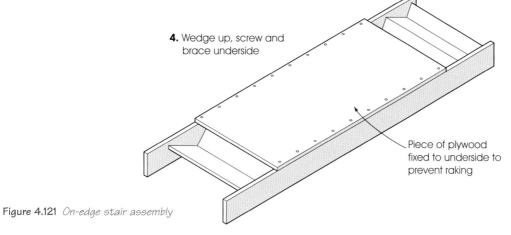

Figure 4.121 *On-edge stair assembly*

Manufacture of Joinery Products

Chapter 4

Cut string stairs

Figure 4.122 shows the construction details of a cut-and-bracketed string. This type is used as the outer string of decorative flights. The string is cut to the shape of the step and the treads are pocket screwed to them. The risers extend past the face of the string and are mitred with thin plywood brackets, which are glued and pinned in place.

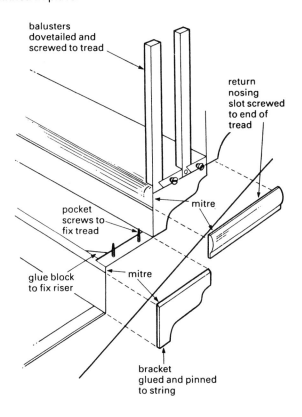

Figure 4.122 *Cut-and-bracketed string*

Most of the assembly will be completed in the workshop with the exception of the following, which will be completed on site: the balusters, which are dovetailed and screwed to the tread, and the return nosings, which are slot screwed to the end of the tread.

Open riser stairs

Figure 4.123 shows a method used to join the treads to the strings in a riserless flight of stairs (open plan). The through tenons should be wedged on the outside of the string. Alternatively, the treads could be simply housed into the string, and metal ties used under every third or fourth tread to tie the flight together.

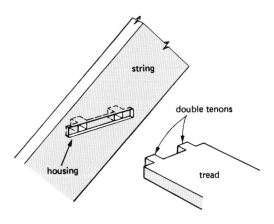

Figure 4.123 *Open riser stair tread to string joint*

Where carriages instead of strings are used in an open-plan flight the treads are supported by two timber brackets, which are either doweled or tenoned into the carriage as shown in Figure 4.124. Alternatively, these may be replaced by purpose-made metal brackets.

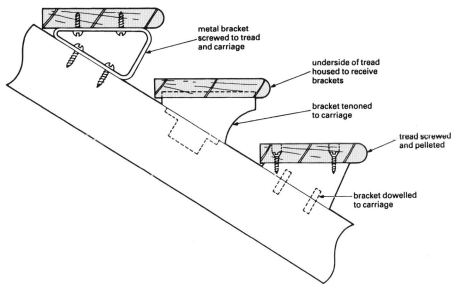

metal bracket screwed to tread and carriage

underside of tread housed to receive brackets

bracket tenoned to carriage

tread screwed and pelleted

bracket dowelled to carriage

Figure 4.124 *Alternative bracket details for stairs with carriages*

On certain flights where the gap between the treads is restricted, a partial riser tongued to either the top or underside of the tread can be used to reduce the gap. Figure 4.125 illustrates these two alternative methods. A third method, which can be used to reduce the gap, is to insert metal rods or large timber dowels from string to string midway between each tread.

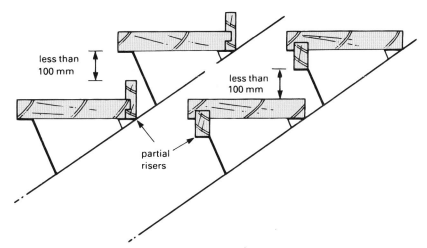

less than 100 mm

less than 100 mm

partial risers

Figure 4.125 *Use of partial risers to reduce gap*

Alternating tread stairs

These are a form of open-riser stair with paddle-shaped treads. One part of the tread is cut away, with the wide portion alternating from one side to the other on each consecutive tread. They should only be used to give access to one room of a domestic loft conversion, where there is insufficient space to accommodate a proper staircase. In addition a handrail should be fitted to both sides and the treads should have a non-slip surface.

Units and fitments

Units fall into two distinct categories.

1. *Purpose-made* – a unit made in a joiners shop for a specific job. Most will be fully assembled prior to their arrival on site.
2. *Proprietary* – a unit or range of units mass produced to standard designs by a manufacturer. Budget-priced units are often sent in knock-down form (known as flat packs) ready for on-site assembly. Better quality units are often ready assembled (known as rigid units) in the factory.

did you know?

Knock down or flat-pack units are also termed KD units.

Unit terminology

Cupboard – historically derived from the name given to the simple open boards or shelves that were used to display cups, silverplate and other items (cup board).

Carcass – the main assembly or frames of a cupboard, excluding doors and drawers.

Potboard – the lower shelf or base of a cupboard. Again, historically derived from the name given to a low board or shelf, raised just off the floor on which heavy cooking pots were stored.

did you know?

The end standards of a unit may also be termed 'gables' and the intermediate standards as 'haffits' (meaning 'half of it' or 'half way').

Plinth – the recessed base of a cupboard, which supports the potboard. It also provides a footspace for those standing in front of the cupboard and is often called a kickboard.

Standards – the vertical end frames or panels and intermediate divisions of a cupboard.

The two main methods of carcass construction for both proprietary and purpose-made units, shown in Figure 4.126, are box construction and framed construction.

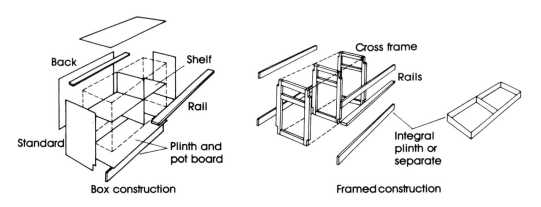

Figure 4.126 *Unit construction*

Box construction

This is also known as **slab construction**. It uses vertical standards and rails and horizontal shelves.

A back holds the unit square and rigid. The plinth and potboard are often integral with the unit.

Proprietary units are almost exclusively made from 15 mm to 19 mm thick melamine-faced chipboard (MFC) or melamine-faced medium-density fibre board (MF MDF).

Purpose-made units may be constructed using MFC, MF MDF, blockboard, plywood or, more rarely, solid timber.

Flat packs use knock-down fittings or screws to join the panels. Assembly is a simple process of following the manufacturer's instructions and drawings, coupled with the ability to use a screwdriver. See Figure 4.127.

Rigid and purpose-made units may be either dowelled or housed and screwed together. Glue is used on assembly to form a rigid carcass. Typical carcass construction details are illustrated in Figure 4.128.

Framed construction

This is also known as **skeleton construction**. This uses frames either front and back joined by rails or standards, or cross frames joined by rails. The plinth and potboard are normally separate items.

The frames of proprietary units are normally dowelled, whereas purpose-made ones would be mortised and tenoned together. Typical carcass construction details are illustrated in Figure 4.129.

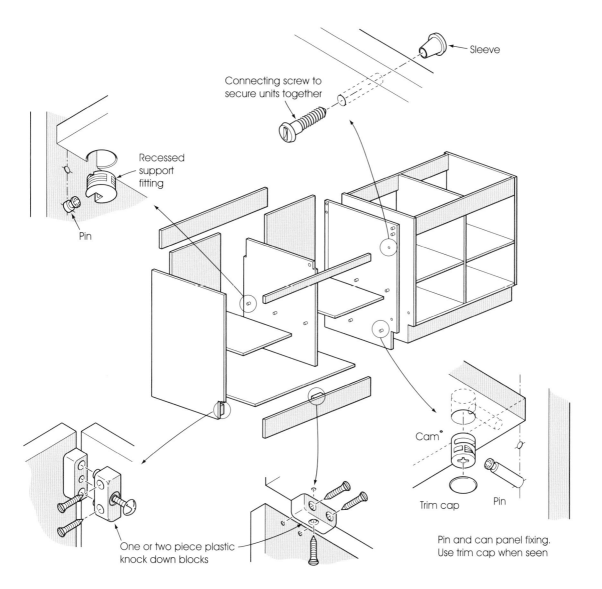

Figure 4.127 *Box construction unit typical knock-down fittings*

Manufacture of Joinery Products

Chapter 4

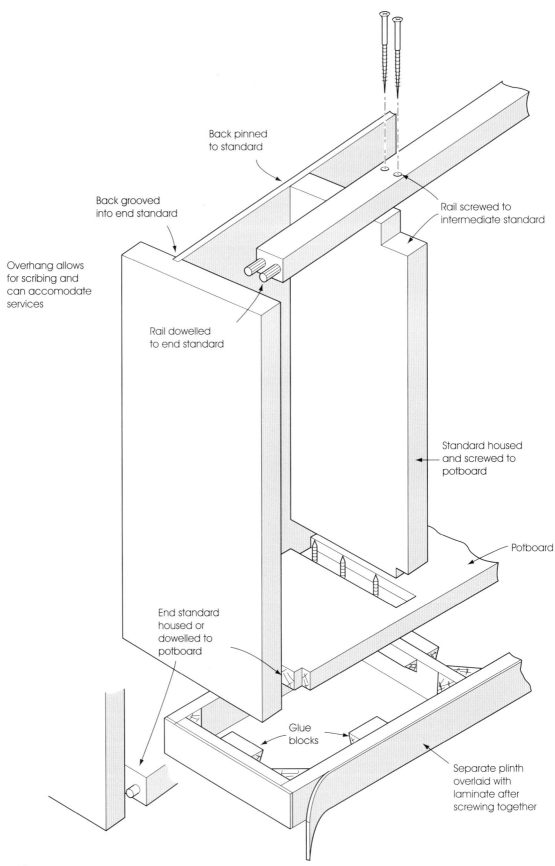

Back pinned
to standard

Back grooved
into end standard

Rail screwed to
intermediate standard

Overhang allows
for scribing and
can accomodate
services

Rail dowelled
to end standard

Standard housed
and screwed to
potboard

Potboard

End standard
housed or
dowelled to
potboard

Glue
blocks

Separate plinth
overlaid with
laminate after
screwing together

Figure 4.128 *Rigid box construction*

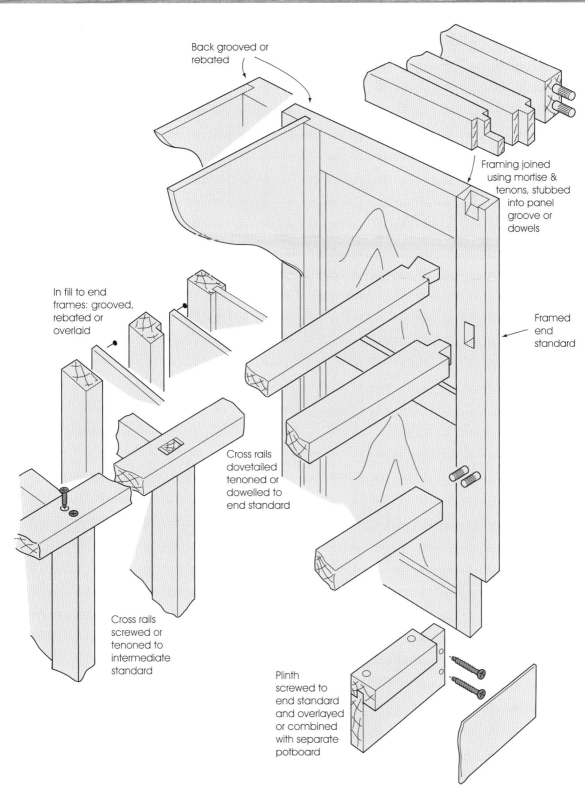

Back grooved or rebated

Framing joined using mortise & tenons, stubbed into panel groove or dowels

In fill to end frames: grooved, rebated or overlaid

Framed end standard

Cross rails dovetailed tenoned or dowelled to end standard

Cross rails screwed or tenoned to intermediate standard

Plinth screwed to end standard and overlayed or combined with separate potboard

Figure 4.129 *Framed unit construction details*

Manufacture of Joinery Products

Chapter 4

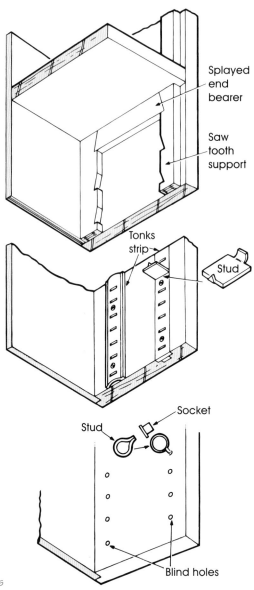

Figure 4.130 *Adjustable shelf details*

Adjustable shelves

In situations where the sizes of the items to be stored are not known or where they are subject to change, some form of shelf adjustment must be incorporated.

Three of the many methods used are listed below and illustrated in Figure 4.130:

◆ The traditional solution was the use of saw tooth supports and splayed end push-in shelf bearers, which can be fitted at any desired height.
◆ A very popular and efficient method is the use of 'tonks': bookcase strips and studs, which allow height adjustment in 25 mm units. The flush strip is designed to be recessed into the standards and a smaller, deeper groove must also be run to give clearance for inserting the tongues of the studs. Alternatively, a surface-fixed strip can be used. This overcomes the need for grooving out and weakening members, but results in an inferior finish as there will be a larger gap between the standards and the ends of the shelves.
◆ Sockets tapped into blind holes that have been drilled at intervals down the standards, and used with push-in studs, are suitable for a lighter range of applications.

Drawers

Drawers may be incorporated into units in order to provide storage and security (when fitted with a lock) for smaller items. The size of a drawer will be related to the items it is intended to store, but in general will range between 100 mm and 200 mm in depth. When they are vertically stacked in one unit the deeper drawers should be located at the bottom.

Figure 4.131 illustrates a traditional method of drawer construction that uses through dovetails at the back and lapped dovetails at the front. The plywood bottom is grooved into the front and sides and is pinned to the bottom of the drawer back. Small glue blocks are positioned under the bottom to provided additional rigidity and assist sliding. Rounded machine-made dovetails, produced on a router or spindle moulder, are a more economic alternative for better quality work where repetitive production is required.

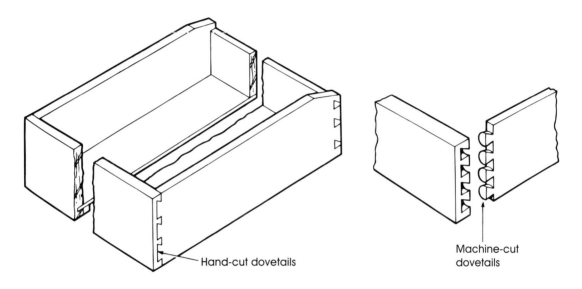

Hand-cut dovetails

Machine-cut dovetails

Figure 4.131 *Traditional drawer construction*

Manufacture of Joinery Products

Chapter 4

Modern mass-produced drawers are made in MFC or MDF. The corner joints can be housed and pinned, butted and screwed, dowelled or biscuited. The bottom of the drawer is typically either nailed or screwed directly to the underside of the drawer sides. A separate false slab front is secured to the drawer by screws from the inside as illustrated in Figure 4.132.

Various methods can be used to suspend and slide drawers. Figure 4.133 shows how traditionally rails may be incorporated into a unit for this purpose. The dustboard shown grooved into the rails is used mainly on better quality work. Its purpose is to separate the drawer and cupboard spaces. A drawer kicker is fitted between the top rails to prevent the front of the drawer falling downwards as it is pulled out. When closed, the drawer front should finish flush with the unit. This can be achieved by pinning small plywood drawer stops to the front of the drawer rail.

Another traditional method of suspending and sliding drawers is shown in Figure 4.134. This uses grooved drawer sides, preferably of a hardwood with good wearing qualities, which slide on hardwood runners glued and screwed to the unit's sides or standards. Where this method is used, the drawer is often fitted with a false slab front screwed from the inside of the drawer. This front has projecting ends to conceal the runner from view. Alternatively, fibre drawer slides may be used (see Figure 4.135). One part is fixed to the side of the drawer and the other to the unit.

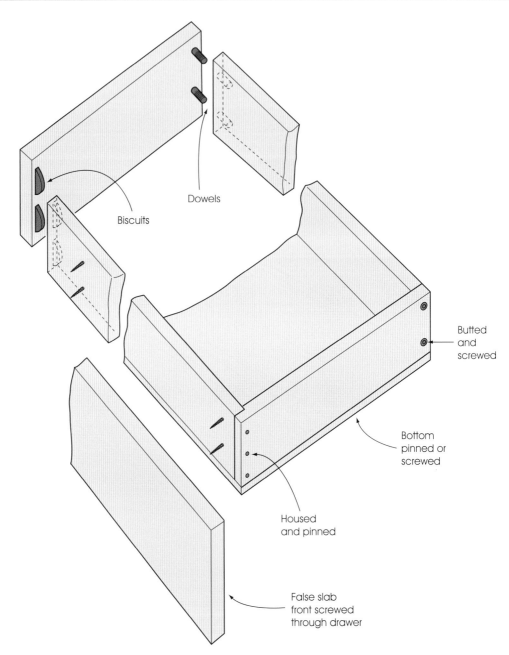

Dowels

Biscuits

Butted and screwed

Bottom pinned or screwed

Housed and pinned

False slab front screwed through drawer

Figure 4.132 *Modern drawer construction*

Modern methods of suspending and sliding drawers, shown in Figure 4.136, employ the use of metal, side or bottom mounted runners. These incorporate a ball race or plastic rollers to ensure ease of operation.

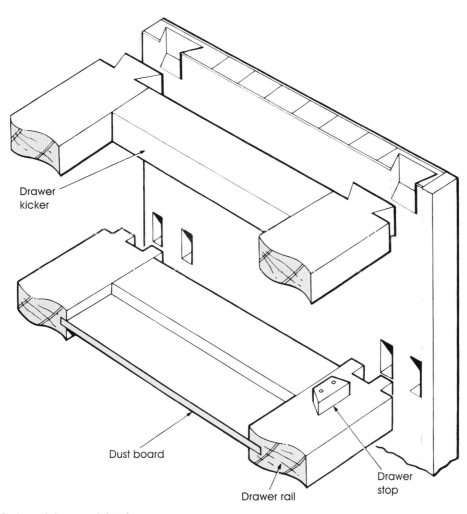

Drawer
kicker

Dust board

Drawer rail

Drawer
stop

Figure 4.133 *Traditional drawer rail details*

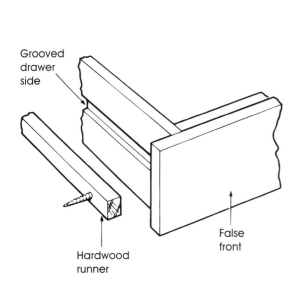

Grooved
drawer
side

Hardwood
runner

False
front

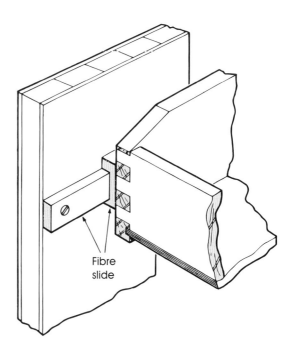

Fibre
slide

Figure 4.134 *Traditional drawer slide detail*

Figure 4.135 *Fibre drawer slides*

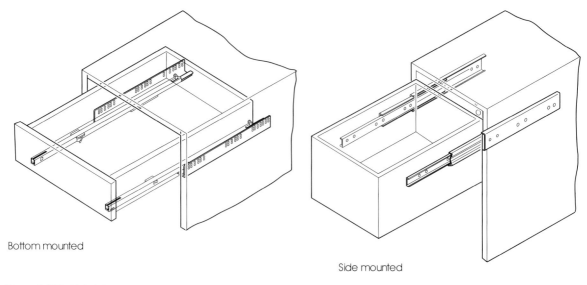

Bottom mounted

Side mounted

Figure 4.136 *Metal drawer runners*

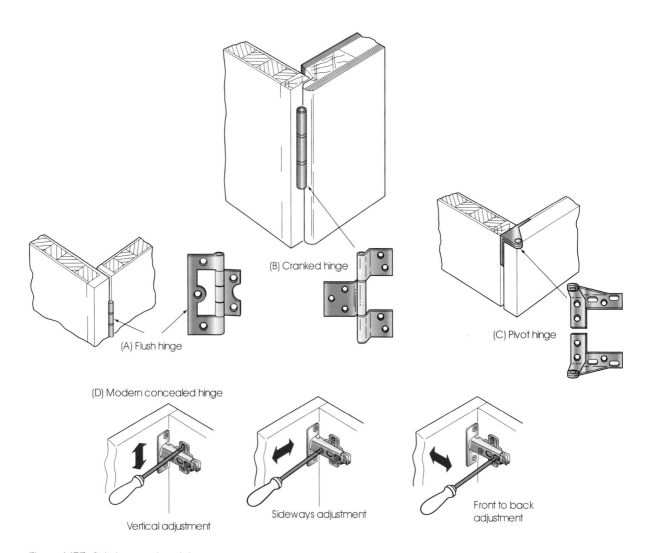

(A) Flush hinge

(B) Cranked hinge

(C) Pivot hinge

(D) Modern concealed hinge

Vertical adjustment

Sideways adjustment

Front to back adjustment

Figure 4.137 *Side-hung cupboard doors*

Doors

Doors can be incorporated to close the front of open units for reasons of tidiness, protection or security. They may be either side-hung or sliding doors. Side-hung doors allow maximum access but when they are open, they project into the room, which can be restrictive and even hazardous in confined spaces. Figure 4.137 illustrates the following various methods of side-hanging cupboard doors:

(A) The door is set flush within the unit and hung on butt hinges. The use of flush hinges avoids the need for recessing and provides the necessary clearance joint.

(B) Rebated doors hung on cranked hinges were at one time popular for mass-produced units. These doors do not require any individual fitting as the rebate, which laps over the face of the unit, conceals the very large clearance joint.

(C) Doors hung on the face of a unit are probably the simplest to make and fit. Although this arrangement is possible with standard butt hinges, the use of cranked or special extended pivot hinges permits the door to open within the width of the unit.

(D) Doors are again face hung. A **concealed cabinet hinge** is bored into the rear face of the door and its mounting plate fixed to the inside of the standard. This type, which is extensively used in modern kitchen units, allows the door to be adjusted in height, sideways, backwards and forward. They include a degree of self-closing in the final stage of swing and do not require a catch.

There are various methods available for making cupboard doors slide. Glass, thin plywood or MDF doors are often made to slide in nylon or fibre tracks (see Figure 4.138). The deeper channel track is used at the top, so the doors can be inserted and removed by pushing them up into the top track, clearing the bottom one.

Figure 4.139 shows how a cupboard door may be made to slide on fibre tracks grooved into the pot board. Two nylon sliders are recessed and screwed to the underside of each door. These run on the fibre track and provide a smooth sliding action that wears well. The top edge of the door is usually rebated to engage in a groove run in the underside of the top rail. Sufficient clearance for insertion and removal must be made at this point to allow the bottom of the door to clear the pot board when pushed up into the top groove. Retractable top guides similar to flush bolts can be used instead of rebating the top edges of the doors.

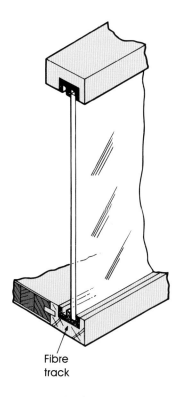

Fibre track

Figure 4.138 *Glass or thin sheet material sliding doors*

Manufacture of Joinery Products

Chapter 4

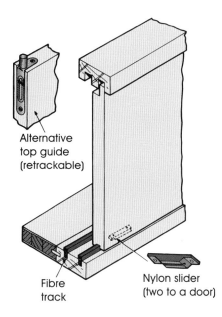

Alternative top guide (retrackable)

Fibre track

Nylon slider (two to a door)

Figure 4.139 *Sliding cupboard doors*

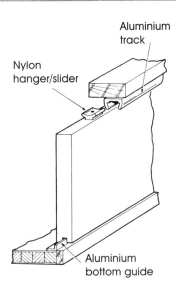

Aluminium track

Nylon hanger/slider

Aluminium bottom guide

Figure 4.140 *Top-hung door*

Heavyweight cupboard doors are best top hung to achieve a smooth running action.

Figure 4.140 illustrates one of the simplest types of top-hung cupboard door sliding track. It consists of a surface-fixed aluminium top track and bottom guide. The door is suspended by two nylon hangers/sliders fixed to its top edge.

The handle position of bottom-sliding doors is best kept nearer the bottom of the door for smooth sliding action. There will be a tendency for the door to tip and judder if the handle is positioned higher than a distance equal to the doors width. The best action is achieved with top-hung doors when the handle position is kept as high as possible.

Worktops

The main types in common use are illustrated in Figure 4.141.

> **did you know?**
>
> A balancer applied to the reverse face of a laminated or veneered board to prevent distortion may also be called a 'compensator'.

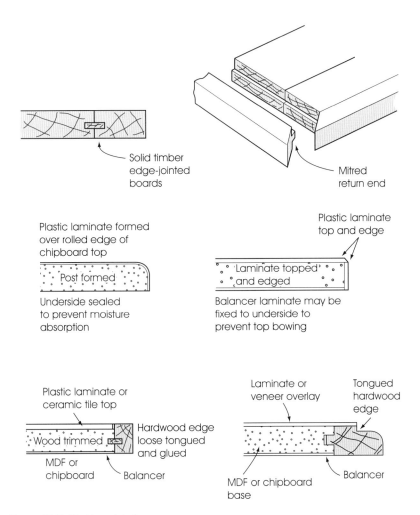

Solid timber edge-jointed boards

Mitred return end

Plastic laminate formed over rolled edge of chipboard top

Post formed

Underside sealed to prevent moisture absorption

Plastic laminate top and edge

'Laminate topped' and edged

Balancer laminate may be fixed to underside to prevent top bowing

Plastic laminate or ceramic tile top

Wood trimmed

Hardwood edge loose tongued and glued

MDF or chipboard

Balancer

Laminate or veneer overlay

Tongued hardwood edge

MDF or chipboard base

Balancer

Figure 4.141 *Worktop details*

Solid timber – made up from narrow-edge jointed boards. Provision for moisture movement needs to be considered when fixing them to a carcass. Mitred return ends may be specified; these serve to hold the top flat and also cover the exposed end grain.

Post-formed – a chipboard base covered with a plastic laminate that has been formed over a rolled edge. This is ready finished and simply requires fixing in place, so it the most popular type of worktop for kitchen units.

Edged sheet material – a chipboard or MDF base covered with either a melamine face, plastic laminate or wood veneer. Matching edging is applied to the seen edges. The undersides of sheet material tops should be the same as the topface or be sealed to prevent distortion. It is good practice to use a double faced, melamine or wood veneer board. On good quality work a balancer laminate is applied to the underside of laminate faced tops to relieve the stresses that would result from facing one side only. A cheaper alternative is to seal the underside with an application of varnish or adhesive.

Wood trimmed – a chipboard or MDF base covered with either melamine face, plastic laminate or wood veneer. A hardwood lipping or edging is simply glued; rebated, glued and screwed; or tongued and glued to the seen edges, providing a neat finish. Return corners are better mitred than butted.

Wood trimmed and overlaid – a chipboard or MDF base edged in hardwood and overlaid with either laminate or wood veneer. The laminate is trimmed off on the spindle moulder or by use of a hand held power router. Often a decorative edge feature is incorporated in the trimming process.

Built-in fitments

These normally use the wall, floor and/or ceiling as part of the construction.

Cupboards – Figure 4.142 shows details of a cupboard that is built into a reveal at the side of a fireplace. It has been framed up using 38mm × 75mm framing.

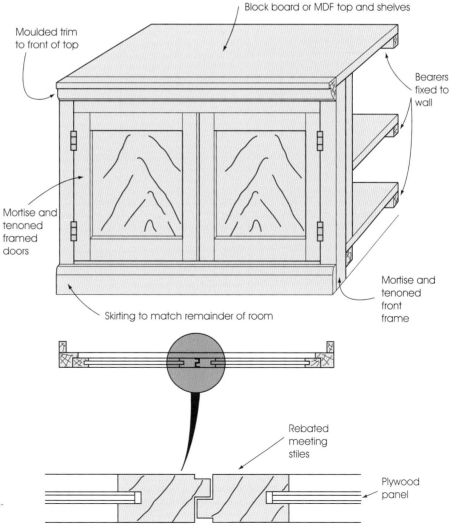

Block board or MDF top and shelves

Moulded trim to front of top

Bearers fixed to wall

Mortise and tenoned framed doors

Mortise and tenoned front frame

Skirting to match remainder of room

Rebated meeting stiles

Plywood panel

Figure 4.142 *Framed front built-in fitment*

The skirting is continued across the front of the frame to match in with the existing timber work. The doors, which have rebated meeting stiles, are also framed up and a 9mm plywood is used for the panels. The top, base, shelf and front framework are fixed to 25mm × 50mm battens that have been plugged and screwed to the walls.

Wardrobes – shown in Figure 4.143 is a plan, elevation and section of a 'built-in' wardrobe. This can be made up using 18 or 25mm MFC or MDF for the base, partitions, shelves and doors.

Manufacture of Joinery Products

Chapter 4

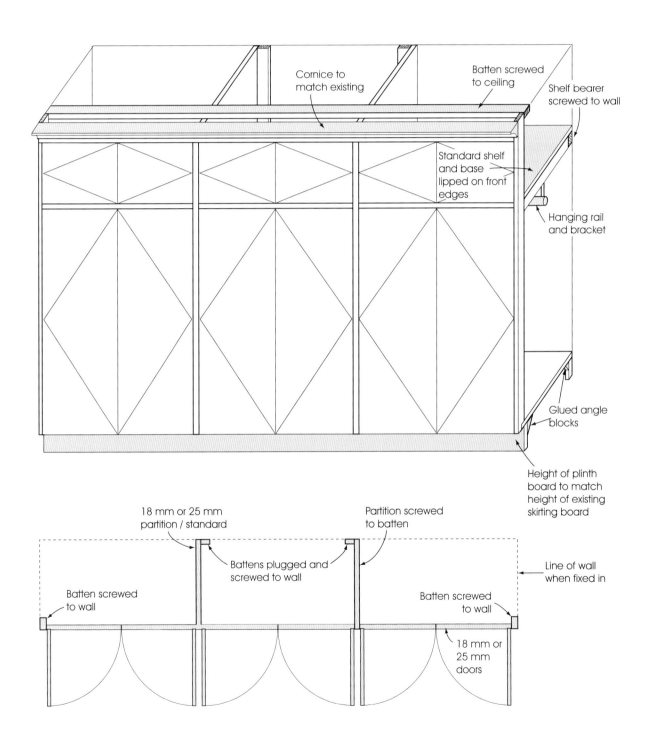

Figure 4.143 *Built-in wardrobe*

To provide a good finish, the exposed edges should be either lipped with 10 mm timber edging or be taped with an iron-on edging. See Figure 4.144.

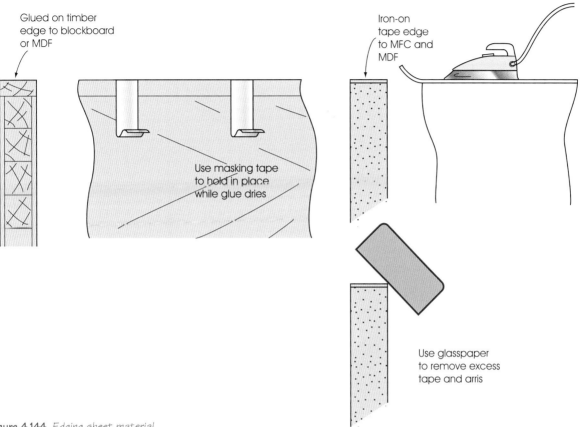

Glued on timber edge to blockboard or MDF

Use masking tape to hold in place while glue dries

Iron-on tape edge to MFC and MDF

Use glasspaper to remove excess tape and arris

Figure 4.144 *Edging sheet material*

The outside doors are hung on 25 mm × 50 mm battens which have been fixed to the walls, while all the remaining doors are hung on the partitions. These can be hung inside the opening using flush hinges, or on the face using concealed cabinet hinges.

The base is made up on a plinth board to match the height of the existing skirting as shown. An infill piece is used at the top to drop the head of the wardrobe down, so that a cornice to match the existing one can be fixed along the ceiling line if required.

Table construction

Details of a typical table suitable for use in most situations is illustrated in Figure 4.145. The table consists of four legs that are joined by four rails. The joint shown in Figure 4.146 between the rails and legs is a table haunched mortise and tenon.

The tenon is bare-faced and is mitred on its end to allow for the tenon of the other rail. Alternatively, dowels, biscuits or proprietary brackets may be used for the leg-to-rail joints. Also illustrated are different methods, used for fixing the table top to the framework. Pocket screwing and plastic blocks are suitable for sheet material whereas the other methods allow for moisture movement when solid timber tops are used.

Assembly procedure for units and fitments

The assembly of framed items follows closely that of other framed joinery items.

The following procedure is illustrated in Figure 4.147.

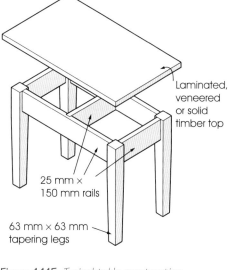

Laminated, veneered or solid timber top

25 mm × 150 mm rails

63 mm × 63 mm tapering legs

Figure 4.145 *Typical table construction*

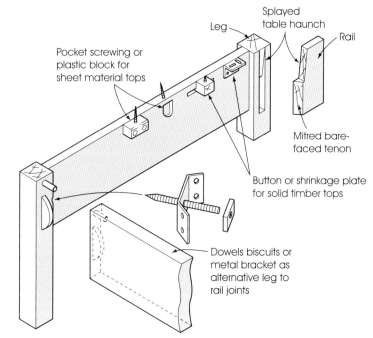

Pocket screwing or plastic block for sheet material tops

Leg

Splayed table haunch

Rail

Mitred bare-faced tenon

Button or shrinkage plate for solid timber tops

Dowels biscuits or metal bracket as alternative leg to rail joints

Figure 4.146 *Table jointing details*

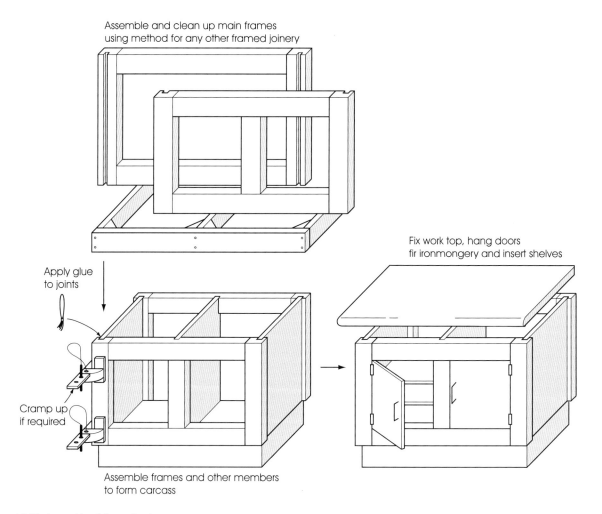

Assemble and clean up main frames using method for any other framed joinery

Fix work top, hang doors fir ironmongery and insert shelves

Apply glue to joints

Cramp up if required

Assemble frames and other members to form carcass

Figure 4.147 *Assembly of framed units*

1. Dry assemble to check fit of joints, overall sizes, square and winding.
2. Clean up inside edges of all framing components and both faces of infill panels, etc.
3. Glue, assemble, cramp up and wedge each individual frame. Re-check for square and winding.
4. Clean up internal faces of individual frames.
5. Clean up any rails, shelves, top and potboard, etc.
6. Glue, assemble and cramp up individual frames and other members to form the unit carcass. Check for square.
7. Clean up external surfaces and prepare for finishing.
8. Fix worktop if separate.
9. Install drawers, hang doors and fix any ironmongery.

The assembly of box construction units can be carried out using the following procedure (shown in Figure 4.148).

1. Check measurement of panels.
2. Carry out any necessary handwork, such as squaring out corners, iron-on edging, fittings for shelves and drawers, etc.
3. Where proprietary knock-down fittings are being used, these should be pre-fitted to each panel at this stage.
4. Assemble panels, use glue and cramps if required.
5. Fix worktop if separate.
6. Install drawers, hang doors, fix any ironmongery and insert any shelving.

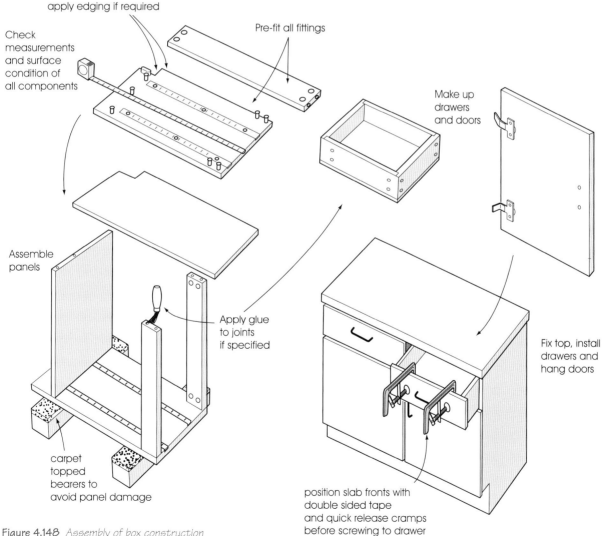

Square out corners and apply edging if required

Check measurements and surface condition of all components

Pre-fit all fittings

Make up drawers and doors

Assemble panels

Apply glue to joints if specified

carpet topped bearers to avoid panel damage

Fix top, install drawers and hang doors

position slab fronts with double sided tape and quick release cramps before screwing to drawer

Figure 4.148 *Assembly of box construction*

Manufacture of Joinery Products

Chapter 4

Study the method statement and data sheet shown in Figure 4.149 for any irregularities. Write a memo or email seeking clarification, if required, from Mark Wood, the setter/marker-out responsible for the job.

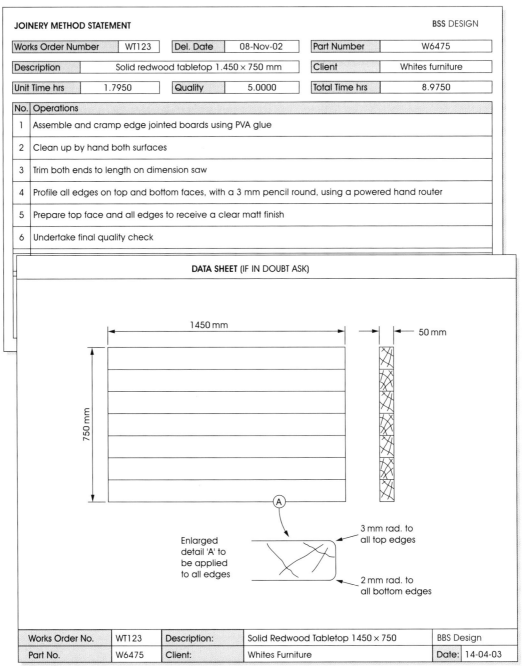

JOINERY METHOD STATEMENT   **BSS** DESIGN

Works Order Number	WT123	Del. Date	08-Nov-02	Part Number	W6475
Description		Solid redwood tabletop 1.450 × 750 mm		Client	Whites furniture
Unit Time hrs	1.7950	Quality	5.0000	Total Time hrs	8.9750

No.	Operations
1	Assemble and cramp edge jointed boards using PVA glue
2	Clean up by hand both surfaces
3	Trim both ends to length on dimension saw
4	Profile all edges on top and bottom faces, with a 3 mm pencil round, using a powered hand router
5	Prepare top face and all edges to receive a clear matt finish
6	Undertake final quality check

DATA SHEET (IF IN DOUBT ASK)

1450 mm

50 mm

750 mm

A

Enlarged detail 'A' to be applied to all edges

3 mm rad. to all top edges

2 mm rad. to all bottom edges

Works Order No.	WT123	Description:	Solid Redwood Tabletop 1450 × 750	BBS Design	
Part No.	W6475	Client:	Whites Furniture	Date:	14-04-03

Figure 4.149 *Method statement and data sheet*

21. Describe or sketch the difference between box and frame unit construction.

22. Produce a sketch to show the following THREE worktop edge details:
(a) post-formed;
(b) wood trimmed;
(c) wood trimmed with laminate overlay.

23. Explain the purpose of a balancer when laminating sheet material.

24. The vertical member used to form a step is a:
(a) tread;
(b) string;
(c) riser;
(d) newel.

25. Explain the term 'going' when applied to stairs.

26. Define the abbreviations MFC and MDF.

27. Produce sketches to show the difference between traditional and modern methods of drawer construction.

28. List the main sequence of operation for assembling a straight flight of stairs, 'closed' on both sides.

29. Glass sliding doors are to be fitted in a book display unit, using a plastic channel track. Explain why the channels for the top and bottom are of a different section.

30. Sketch or describe TWO methods of providing, adjustable height shelf supports.

Manufacture of Joinery Products

Chapter 4

5 Circular Saws

This chapter is intended to provide the reader with an overview of setting up and using circular saws in both a workshop and on-site situation. Its contents are assessed in the **NVQ Unit VR 13 Set Up and Use Circular Saws.**

In this chapter you will cover the following range of topics:

◆ legislation and guidance;
◆ accident statistics;
◆ types of circular saw;
◆ safe working practices for circular saws;
◆ tooling;
◆ maintenance;
◆ troubleshooting.

What is required in VR 13?

To successfully complete this unit you will be required to demonstrate your skill and knowledge of the following processes:

◆ Interpreting information;
◆ Adopting safe and healthy working practices;
◆ Selecting materials, components and equipment;
◆ Setting up, using and maintaining circular saws in accordance with current legislation and official guidance.

You will be required practically to:

◆ use fixed or transportable circular saws and appropriate aids to:
  ▶ cut timber and timber manufactured sheet material
  ▶ change saw blades;
◆ use appropriate personal protective equipment to carry out an activity;
◆ maintain a clean work area and safely dispose of waste material;
◆ identify problems associated with the use of circular saws;
◆ communicate with other team members;
◆ undertake calculations for quantity, length, area and wastage.

Legislation and guidance

Practical guidance on safe working practices to be observed when using woodworking machines is contained in an Approved Code of Practice (ACOP) *Safe Use of Woodworking Machinery.* This ACOP takes into account both the practical aspects of machine safety and the legal requirements contained in the Provision and Use of Work Equipment Regulations (PUWER) and the Management of Health and Safety at Work Regulations (MHSW). In addition, the Health and Safety Executive produce a series of *wood information sheets*, which contain further practical guidance on the safe use of individual woodworking machines. These may be viewed on this website: www.hse.gov.uk.

Circular Saws

Chapter 5

> **did you know?**
>
> Duties in legislation can be either be **absolute** or have a qualifying term added called **reasonably practicable**.
>
> ▸ **Absolute** – unless a qualifying term is added such as **whenever reasonably practicable**, the requirement must be met regardless of cost or any other consideration.
>
> ▸ **Reasonably practicable** – means that you are required to consider the risks involved in undertaking a particular work activity. However, if the risks are minimal and the cost or technical difficulties of taking certain actions to eliminate the risks are very high, it might not be reasonably practicable to take those actions.

The main general requirements to be considered wherever woodworking machines are to be used may be summarised under the following headings:

Use of safety appliances

◆ The use of safety appliances, such as push sticks and jigs, keep the operator's hands in a safe positions, whilst allowing the operator to maintain full control of the workpiece during cutting operations.
◆ Power feeds reduce the need for hands to approach the cutters and should be used whenever reasonably practicable.

Machine controls

◆ All machines should be fitted with a means of isolation from the electric supply, which should be located close to the machine.
◆ Lockable isolators can be used to prevent unauthorised use of a machine and give increased protection during maintenance.

Working space

◆ Machines should be located in such a position that the operator cannot be pushed, bumped or easily distracted.
◆ There should be sufficient space around machines for the items to be machined, for finished workpieces and for waste bins, so that there is no obstruction affecting the operator.
◆ Wherever possible, machine shop areas should be separated from assembly or packaging areas, and from areas used by forklift trucks or other forms of transportation.
◆ All access and escape routes must be kept clear.
◆ Waste bins should be emptied at regular intervals and waste sacks containing wood dust should be stored outside the workroom.

Floors

◆ The floor surface of the work area must be level, non-slip and maintained in good condition.
◆ The working area around a machine must be kept free from obstruction, off-cuts and shavings, etc.
◆ Supply cables and pipes should be routed at high level or set below floor level, in order to prevent a tripping or trapping hazard.
◆ Polished floors should be avoided as they present a risk of slipping.
◆ All spillages should be promptly cleared up to avoid the risk of slipping.

Lighting

◆ Machinists require good lighting (natural or artificial) in order to operate safely.
◆ Lighting should be positioned or shaded to prevent glare and not shine in the operator's eyes.
◆ Adequate lighting must also be provided for gangways and passages.
◆ Windows should be shaded when necessary to avoid reflections from worktables and other shiny surfaces.

Heating

◆ Low temperatures can result in a loss of concentration and cold hands can reduce the operator's ability to control the workpiece safely.
◆ A temperature of 16°C is suitable for a machine shop.
◆ In a sawmill where heavier work is undertaken a temperature between 10°C and 16°C is considered suitable.
◆ Where it is not possible to heat the entire area, radiant heaters can be provided near or adjacent to the work area to enable operators to warm themselves periodically.

Dust collection

◆ Wood dust is harmful to health.
◆ Woodworking machines should be fitted with an efficient means of collecting wood dust and chippings.
◆ Local exhaust ventilation systems should be regularly maintained to prevent their efficiency from deteriorating.

Training

◆ Individuals should not use any woodworking machine unless they have been properly trained for the work being carried out.
◆ People under 18 years of age are prohibited from operating certain machines, unless they have successfully completed an approved training course.

Accident statistics

When compared to other industries woodworking accounts for a disproportionately high number of machine accidents. In a Health and Safety Executive (HSE) survey of 1000 woodworking machine accidents circular saw benches accounted for 35% of the total as illustrated by the pie chart in Figure 5.1.

Many of these accidents resulted in the loss of fingers. Of the total for circular saw benches, 83% occurred whilst undertaking ripping or crosscutting operations. In most cases the saw guard was either incorrectly adjusted or missing altogether.

The HSE states that many of the accidents could have been avoided if the saw guard was correctly adjusted and a push stick used.

The HSE statistics go on to show that accidents are disproportionately high in premises that employ a smaller number of people as illustrated in Figure 5.2. Over 50% of those injured had only received 'on-the-job training'; 24% had not received training or instruction on the machine they were using and of these only 5% were under supervision; finally 25% of accidents involved formally trained operators, which indicates that safe working methods were being bypassed.

Risks must be controlled by:

▶ **eliminating the risk** – or if that is not possible:

▶ **taking hardware measures** such as the **provision of guards** to control the risks; but if the risks cannot be adequately controlled:

▶ **taking software measures** such as **following safe systems of work** and the provision of information, instruction and training to deal with the remaining risk.

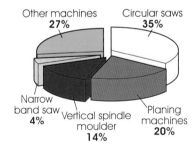

Figure 5.1 *HSE survey of woodworking machine accidents*

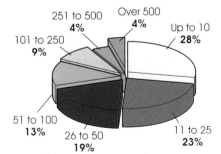

Figure 5.2 *HSE statistics showing percentage of accidents by size of firm*

To help prevent accidents at woodworking machines all concerned should:

◆ Assess all the risks in the workplace and put precautions in place to eliminate them.
◆ Ensure all necessary guards are in position and used at all times.
◆ Ensure all machine operators are suitably trained on the machine they are using and, in addition, ensure that they are properly supervised.
◆ Check that machine operators are following safe working methods at all times.

Types of circular saw

The three main types of circular saw are:

1. **Cross-cut saw** – used for cutting to length.
2. **Rip saw** – used for cutting to width and thickness.
3. **Dimension saw** – used for the precision cutting of timber and sheet material.

There are two basic types of sawing operation as illustrated in Figure 5.3. In the first, used for cross cutting only, the material, which is being cut remains stationary on the table while the revolving saw is drawn across it. The second type, where the material is fed past the revolving saw, is suitable for both rip and cross cutting.

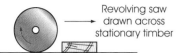
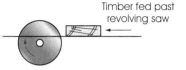

Revolving saw drawn across stationary timber

Timber fed past revolving saw

Figure 5.3 *Circular saw (basic methods)*

Cross-cut saw

The saw unit is drawn across the material, cutting it to length (Figure 5.4).

Adjustable length stops may be fitted where repetitive cutting to the same length is required.

With most models it is also possible to carry out the following operations (see Figure 5.5):

- cross cutting;
- compound cutting;
- cutting birdsmouths;
- cutting housings;
- cutting notches;
- cutting halving joints;
- kerfing;
- ripping (with riving knife fitted);
- trenching, tenoning and ploughing with special cutters.

Figure 5.4 *Cross-cut saw*

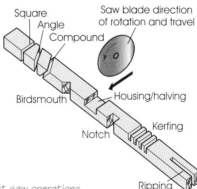

Square
Angle
Compound
Saw blade direction of rotation and travel
Birdsmouth
Housing/halving
Notch
Kerfing
Ripping

Figure 5.5 *Cross-cut saw operations*

Starting, stopping and isolation controls

In common with most woodworking machines, a recessed start button and a mushroom-head stop button control the motor. When connected up, all machines should also be fitted with an isolating switch, so that the machine can be completely isolated (disconnected) from the power supply when setting, adjusting, or carrying out maintenance work on the machine (see Figure 5.6). The purpose of recessing the start button is to prevent accidental switching on. The stop button is mushroomed to aid positive switching off and should be suitably located to enable the operator to switch the machine off with a knee in an emergency.

In addition, to reduce the risk of contact with the operator during the rundown, machines should be fitted with a braking device that brings blades and cutters safely to rest within 10 seconds.

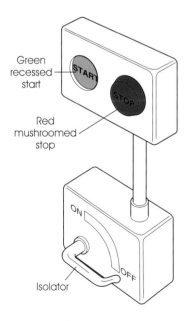

Green recessed start

Red mushroomed stop

Isolator

Figure 5.6 *Start, stop and isolation controls*

Circular Saws **Chapter 5**

Rip saw

The material is fed past the revolving blade on the rip saw to cut it to the required section (see Figure 5.7).

Two main operations are involved in cutting timber to the required section (as illustrated in Figure 5.8):

Figure 5.7 *Rip saw*

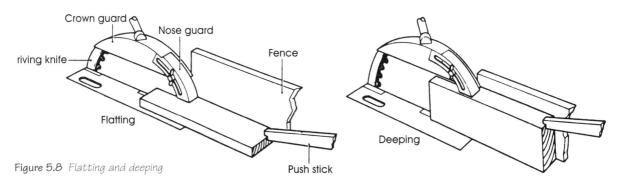

Figure 5.8 *Flatting and deeping*

1. Cutting the timber to the required width, which is known as flatting.
2. Cutting the timber to the required thickness, which is known as deeping.

In addition to flatting and deeping, a third operation may be required as illustrated in Figure 5.9.

3. Cutting the timber to the appropriate bevel, taper or wedge shape. Machine operators often make up their own saddles, bed pieces and jigs to enable them to safely carry out bevel, angle and taper cutting.

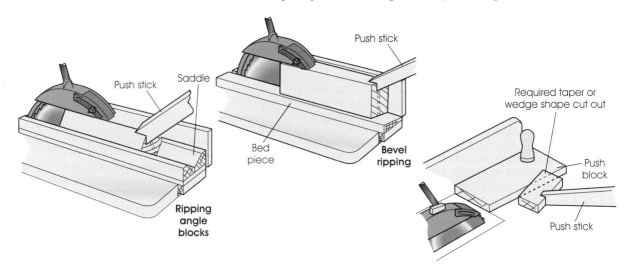

Figure 5.9 *Bed pieces, saddles and jigs*

Some saws have a recess on each side and in front of the blade where it enters the table. These recesses are intended to receive felt packings and a hardwood mouthpiece. The packing helps to keep the saw cutting in a true line. The mouthpiece helps to prevent the underside of the timber breaking out or 'spelching'.

When setting the machine up for any ripping operation, the fence should be adjusted so that the arc on its end is in line with the gullets of the saw teeth at table level. Binding will occur if it is too far forward and, if it is too far back, the material will jump at the end of the cut, leaving a small projection.

Dimension saw

This is used for cutting timber and sheet material to precise dimensions (see Figure 5.10). Most sawing operations are possible although on a lighter scale than the previous two machines.

Dimension saws are also referred to as 'panel saws'.

Figure 5.10 Dimension saw

The cross-cut fence, when fitted, adjusts for angles and the blade may be tilted for bevels/compound cutting and can be moved up and down. The large sliding side table, used for cross cutting, also serves to give support when cutting sheet material.

Circular Saws   Chapter 5

Safe working practices for circular saws

Cross-cut saws

The guidance applicable to cross-cut saws is illustrated in Figure 5.11 and summarised in the following points:

1. The non-cutting part of the blade must be totally enclosed with a fixed guard, which should extend down to at least the spindle.
2. Guards or a saw housing should be provided so that there is no access to the saw blade when in its rest position.
3. A nose guard should be fitted to prevent contact with the front edge of the blade during cutting and when the saw is at rest.
4. The maximum extension or stroke of the saw should be set so the nose guard cannot extend beyond the front of the saw table.
5. A braking device should be fitted to the machine that brings the blade to rest within 10 seconds, unless there is no risk of contact with the blade during rundown.
6. A fence is required on either side of the cutting line and should be high enough to support the timber being cut. The gap in the fence should be just sufficient to allow the passage of the nose guard. When straight cutting

on a machine that is capable of angled cuts, any excessive gap in the fence should be closed by the use of renewable fence inserts or false fence.

7. It is recommended that 'no hands' areas be marked in yellow hatching on the table 300 mm either side of the blade. Operators should be trained not to hold timber in these areas during cutting operations.

8. Workpiece holders or jigs should be used when cutting small workpieces or narrow sections.

9. Offcuts and woodchips should only be removed when the saw has stopped and is in the rest position; even then it is good practice to use a pushstick rather than the hands.

10. In order to reduce the likelihood of distorted timber binding on the saw causing kickback, any bow should be placed against the bed and any spring against the fence, with packers being used to prevent rocking.

11. Although some machines have the facility to turn the cutting head through 90° to allow rip sawing, a circular saw bench is considered a safer, more suitable option.

12. Jigs and workpiece cramps should be used when undertaking operations such as trenching and the pointing of stakes or pales in order to provide workpiece stability and prevent kickback.

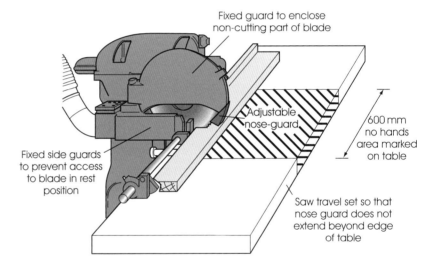

Fixed guard to enclose non-cutting part of blade

Adjustable nose-guard

600 mm no hands area marked on table

Fixed side guards to prevent access to blade in rest position

Saw travel set so that nose guard does not extend beyond edge of table

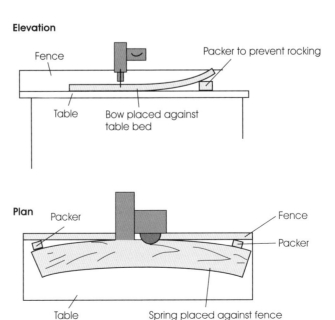

Elevation

Fence

Packer to prevent rocking

Table

Bow placed against table bed

Plan

Packer

Fence

Packer

Table

Spring placed against fence

Figure 5.11 *Safe use of manually operated cross-cut saws*

Circular saw benches

The guidance applicable to circular-saw benches is illustrated in Figure 5.13 (see p. 158) and summarised in the following points:

1. The part of the saw below the saw table must be fully enclosed.
2. In order to reduce the risk of contact with the moving saw blade during rundown a braking device must be fitted to the machine that brings the blade to rest within 10 seconds.
3. A riving knife must be fitted directly behind the saw blade. Its purpose is to part the timber as it proceeds through the saw and thus prevent it jamming on the blade and being thrown back towards the operator. Whenever the saw blade is changed the riving knife must be adjusted so that it is as close as practically possible to the saw blade and, in any case, the distance between the riving knife and the teeth of the saw blade should not exceed 8 mm at table level. The distance between the top of the riving knife and the top of the blade should be no more than 25 mm, except for blades over 600 mm diameter where the riving knife should extend at least 225 mm above the table. Riving knifes should have a chamfered leading edge and be thicker than the saw blade but slightly thinner than the width (kerf) of the saw cut.
4. The upper part of the saw blade must be fitted with a strong adjustable saw guard (crown guard), which has flanges on either side that cover as much of the blade as possible and must be adjusted as close as possible to the workpiece during use. An extension piece (nose guard) may be fitted to the leading end of the crown guard. This guards the blade between the workpiece and crown guard. If when cutting narrow workpieces the guard cannot be lowered sufficiently because it fouls a fixed fence, a false fence should be fitted. In all circumstances the extension piece must be adjusted as close as possible to the workpiece during use.
5. The diameter of the smallest saw blade that can safely be used should be marked on the machine. A smaller blade, less than 60% of the largest saw blade for which the machine is designed, will not cut efficiently due to its lower peripheral (tip of teeth) speed.
6. Saw benches should be fitted with local exhaust ventilation above and below the table, which effectively controls wood dust during the machine's operation.
7. Where an assistant is employed at the outfeed (delivery) end of the machine to remove the cut pieces, an extension table must be fitted so that the distance between the saw blade spindle and the end of the table is at least 1200 mm. The assistant should be instructed to remain at the outfeed end of the extension table and not to reach forward towards the saw blade.
8. The operator's hands should never be in line with the saw blade or be closer than necessary to the front of the saw. A suitable push stick (Figure 5.12) should be used in the following circumstances:
   - feeding material where the cut is 300 mm or less;
   - feeding material over the last 300 mm of the cut;
   - removing cut pieces from between the saw blade and fence unless the width of the cut piece exceeds 150 mm.

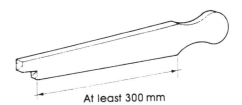

At least 300 mm

Figure 5.12 *Push stick*

9. In order to reduce the risk of contact with the saw blade, it is recommended that a demountable power feed is used whenever possible. This is not a substitute for the riving knife, which must be kept in position at all times.

Circular Saws **Chapter 5**

10. A fence should always be used to give support to the workpiece during cutting. For shallow or angled cutting the normal fence may need replacing with a low fence to enable the use of a push stick or prevent the canted blade touching the fence.

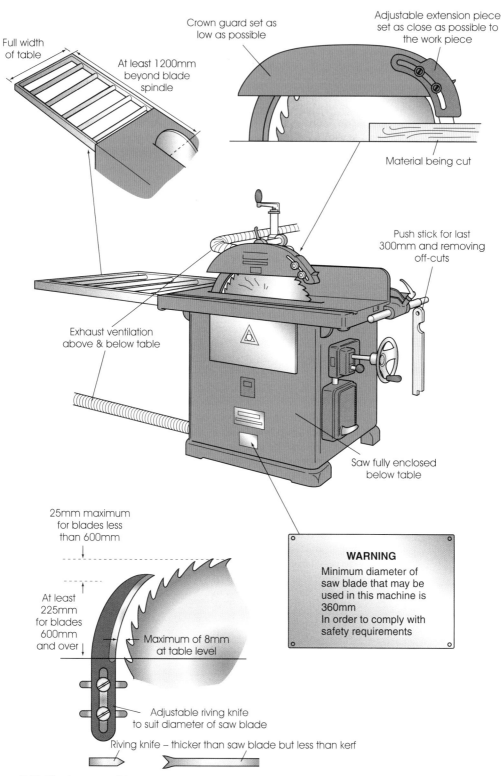

Figure 5.13 *Circular saw safety requirements*

11. The safe working position for the operator is at the feed end offset away from the fence and out of the blade line. See Figure 5.14.

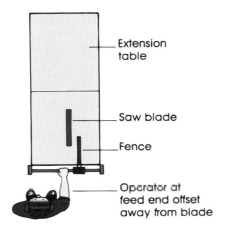

Extension table

Saw blade

Fence

Operator at feed end offset away from blade

Figure 5.14 *Saw operator position*

12. It is recommended that operators wear personal protection (see Figure 5.15): ear protection to reduce the risk of hearing loss; dusk mask or respirator, particularly when cutting hardwoods to reduce the risk of respiratory problems; and goggles or a face screen where there is a risk of flying particles.

| Ear muffs | Dust Mask | Respirator | Goggles | Face screen |

Figure 5.15 *Use personal protection when machining*

13. Circular saws must not be use for the following operations:
- ◆ Cutting tenons, grooves, rebates or mouldings unless effectively guarded. Guards normally take the form of Shaw 'tunnel-type' guards, which, in addition to enclosing the blade, apply pressure to the workpiece, keeping it in place.
- ◆ Ripping is not permissible unless the saw teeth project above the timber, e.g. deeping large sectioned material in two cuts is not allowed.
- ◆ Cutting round section timber unless the workpiece is adequately supported and held by a gripping or cramping device.
- ◆ Angle cuts and bevels can be made on tilting arbour saws by inclining the blade; the fence should be set in the low position or a false fence used to prevent the rotating blade coming into contact with it. On non-tilting fixed position saws bed pieces or jigs can be used to provide workpiece support during cutting.

Circular Saws

Chapter 5

Tooling

A range of **circular saw blades** is available for various types of work. Figure 5.16 illustrates the section of two in common use:

◆ **plate,** also known as **parallel plate,** for straightforward rip and cross cutting work;
◆ **hollow ground** for dimension sawing and fine finished work.

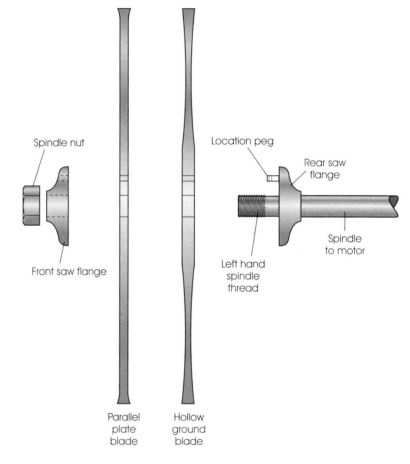

Figure 5.16 *Circular-saw blade section*

Other section blades with a thin rim are available but have limited uses, for example, swage, ground-off and taper. They are used for rip sawing thin sections. Each has its own particular application, although the purpose of each is the same, i.e. to save timber by reducing the width of the saw kerf.

Saw teeth

Saw teeth require setting so that the kerf (width of the saw cut) produced is wider than the thickness of the blade. Otherwise it will bind on the timber and overheat as a result of the friction, causing the blade to wobble and produce a wavy or 'drunken' cut.

The teeth can be set in two main ways, as shown in Figure 5.17:

◆ ***Spring set teeth*** *– where adjacent teeth are sprung to the opposite side of the blade. This is the same method as that used for handsaws.*
◆ ***Swage set teeth*** *– mainly used for setting thin rim rip saws. The point of each tooth is spread out evenly on both sides to give it a dovetail-shaped look.*

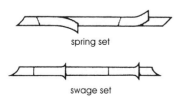

Figure 5.17 *Types of saw blade setting*

did you know?

'TCT' is used as an abbreviation for tungsten carbide tipped saw blades.

Hollow ground and tungsten tipped saws do not require setting as the hollow grinding provides the necessary clearance or the tip side overhang respectively.

Teeth shape

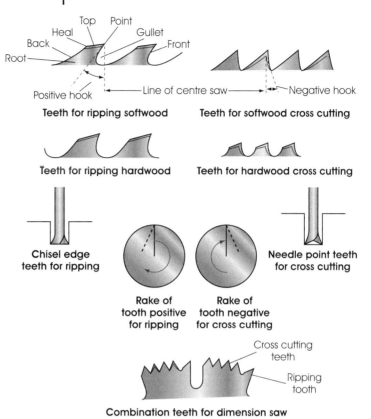

Figure 5.18 *Circular saw teeth*

For efficient cutting the shape of the saw teeth must be suitable for the work being carried out (see Figure 5.18).

◆ *Rip saws* require **chisel-edge teeth**, which incline towards the wood (they have positive hook). Teeth for ripping hardwood require less hook than those for ripping softwood.
◆ *Cross-cut saws* require **needle-point teeth**, which incline away from the wood (they have negative hook). The needle-point teeth for hardwood cross-cutting must be strongly backed up.
◆ *Dimension sawing* ideally requires a **combination blade** of both rip and cross-cut teeth, although, as dimension saw benches are rarely used for ripping, a fine cross-cut blade is often fitted.

Tungsten carbide tips

The use of wear-resistant tungsten carbide tipped teeth saws (Figure 5.19) is recommended when cutting abrasive hardwoods, plywood, MDF and chipboard. Their use reduces excessive blunting of the saw, thus extending the period before blade changing and resharpening is required.

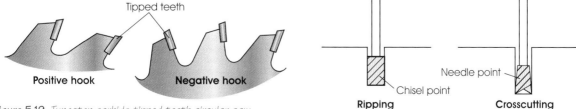

Figure 5.19 *Tungsten carbide-tipped teeth circular saw*

Circular Saws Chapter 5

Maintenance

did you know?

The routine periodic maintenance of a machine is also termed 'preventative maintenance' as, during this work, worn or damaged parts can be identified and replaced before they break down.

Saw blade maintenance

After a period of use, saw blades will start to dull (lose their cutting edge). This will progressively cause a poor finish to the saw cut, including burning of both the timber and the blade and possibly cause blade wobble due to overheating. In addition, it will require excessive pressure by the operator to force the timber through the saw.

The sharpening of circular blades is normally carried out on a saw sharpening machine or by hand filing. However, neither of these operations is within the scope of this Unit of Competence.

To ensure true running of a saw blade, it should be fitted in the same position on the saw spindle each time it is used. This can be achieved by always mounting the blades on the spindle with the location/driving peg uppermost and, before tightening, pulling the saw blade back onto the peg.

Resin deposits on saw blades should be cleaned off periodically. They can be softened by brushing with an oil/paraffin mixture and scraped off. A wood scraper is preferable, as it will avoid scratching the saw blade.

Machine maintenance

Routine periodic maintenance of the machine will:

◆ prolong its serviceable life;
◆ ensure all moving parts work freely;
◆ ensure the machine operates safely.

The manufacturer's maintenance schedule, supplied with each machine, gives the operator information regarding routine maintenance procedures. The schedule will detail the parts to be lubricated, the location of grease nipples and the type, the required frequency and amount of grease.

A typical procedure might be:

1. Remove all rust spots with fine wire wool.
2. Clean off resin deposits and other dirt, using an oil/paraffin mixture and wooden scraper.
3. Wipe over entire machine using clean rag.
4. Apply a coat of light grade oil to all screws and slides. Excess should be wiped off using a clean rag.
5. Clean off grease nipples and apply correct grade and amount of grease using the correct gun. Parts can be rotated manually during this operation.
6. Check freeness of all moving parts.

Troubleshooting

The most common faults that occur when sawing timber along with their probable causes and suggested remedies are listed in Table 5.1.

Table 5.1 Circular sawing: faults, causes, remedies

Fault	Probable cause	Remedy
The saw blade begins to wobble	Saw blade overheating due to: ◆ packing too tight ◆ dull teeth ◆ insufficient set ◆ abrasive timber ◆ loss of tension in saw blade	◆ Reduce thickness of packing ◆ Replace with sharp saw blade ◆ Set teeth ◆ Use tungsten-tipped saw blade ◆ Replace saw blade
The timber being sawn moves away from the fence or binds against the fence	◆ Fence not parallel to saw blade ◆ Arc on fence not set in line with gullets of teeth	◆ Realign fence ◆ Adjust arc of fence to line up with gullets of teeth
Rough sawn finish	◆ Uneven setting or sharpening of teeth	◆ Replace with correctly sharpened and set saw blade
The blade binds in the saw kerf	◆ Dull teeth ◆ Insufficient set ◆ Case hardened or twisted timber	◆ Replace with sharp saw blade ◆ Replace with correctly set saw blade ◆ Avoid if possible; if not, use tungsten-tipped blade and feed slowly forward, easing back when binding occurs
Small projection left at the end of timber after ripping	◆ Arc on fence set too far back from line of gullets, causing the material to jump into gap at end of operation	◆ Realign arc on fence with the saw teeth gullets at table level
Saw cut not square to either table when ripping or fence when crosscutting	◆ Saw blade set at an angle to the table ◆ Cutting head set at an angle to the fence	◆ Adjust inclination of saw blade so that it is at right angles to the table ◆ Adjust cutting head so that it is at right angles to the fence

Circular Saws **Chapter 5**

activity

Consult The Provision and Use of Work Equipment Regulations (PUWER) and the supporting Approved Code of Practice (ACOP) Safe Use of Woodworking Machinery, in order to answer the following questions:

1 List the **three** main duties that the regulations place on employers and the self employed who provide equipment for use at work or persons who control or supervise the use of equipment.
2 Explain what the regulations mean by **hardware and software** measures in relation to the control of risk to peoples health and safety created by the equipment that they use.
3 Describe what the ACOP says about young people and their use of woodworking machinery.
4 Describe what the ACOP says about training. Include in your answer who should be trained and three essential elements of a training scheme.
5 Explain the ACOP requirements under the following headings:
    (a) kickback   (b) disintegration
    (c) stop controls   (d) stability
    (e) markings   (f) warnings.

1. Produce sketches to show the difference between deeping and flatting.

2. Name a type of saw blade that is most suitable for ripping abrasive timber.

3. Describe the safe working position that the operator of a circular hand fed saw bench should take.

4. The riving knife fitted to a circular saw must have a maximum clearance between itself and the blade at table level of:
   (a)   6 mm
   (b)   8 mm
   (c)   10 mm
   (d)   12 mm

5. The guard on a circular saw that covers the top of a saw blade is known as the:
   (a)   shaw guard
   (b)   top guard
   (c)   crown guard
   (d)   bridge guard

6. List **FOUR** general requirements for the safe use of woodworking machines.

7. State **ONE** piece of information that must be fixed to every circular, rip or dimension saw bench.

8. State the purpose of packings to circular saw blades.

9. State why a hardwood mouthpiece may be incorporated in the table of a circular saw bench.

10. Produce a labelled sketch of a circular saw blade tooth indicating six features.

11. State **TWO** reasons for undertaking routine periodic maintenance of woodworking machines.

12 State **TWO** situations where a push stick must be used.

13 List **FIVE** tasks that may be included in the periodic maintenance of a circular saw.

14 Explain why a riving knife thicker than the saw blade should be used.

15 Describe how you would ensure that a saw blade is refitted in exactly the same position after each time it has been taken off for sharpening.

Index

Index